Prayers for Dawn and Dusk

Prayers for Dawn and Dusk

by Edward Francis Gabriele

Saint Mary's Press
Christian Brothers Publications
Winona, Minnesota

The Psalms in this book are from *Psalms Anew: In Inclusive Language*, by Nancy Schreck, OSF, and Maureen Leach, OSF (Winona, MN: Saint Mary's Press, 1986). Copyright © 1986 by Saint Mary's Press. Used with permission. All rights reserved.

The excerpt on pages 11–12 is from *Praying the Psalms*, by Walter Brueggemann (Winona, MN: Saint Mary's Press, 1986). Copyright © 1986 by Saint Mary's Press. All rights reserved.

The publishing team included Carl Koch, FSC, development editor; Mary Duerson Kraemer, copy editor; Amy Schlumpf Manion, production editor; Elaine Kohner, illustrator; cover design by McCormick Creative; pre-press, printing, and binding by the graphics division of Saint Mary's Press.

Printed in the United States of America

Printing: 6 5 4 3 2

Year: 1998 97 96 95 94 93 92

ISBN 0-88489-257-3 paper
    0-88489-275-1 spiral-bound

For Dad and Jimmy as they sing praises now for the Lord;
for Mom, Anita, and my family;
for my Norbertine brothers, especially Fr. Paul Jude O'Hara;
and for all my friends who have taught me
the agony and the ecstasy of what it means to pray

 # Contents

Preface

Originally, the texts found in this work were composed
for the common prayer life of Saint Norbert Abbey
in De Pere, Wisconsin, and my home Norbertine community of Daylesford Abbey in Paoli, Pennsylvania.
The spirit of this book is the liturgy of the hours in the
Roman liturgical tradition. Although this book may be
used by individuals and small communities for the celebration of prayer in the hours of morning and evening,
Prayers for Dawn and Dusk is not a substitute for or an
experiment in the official liturgy of the hours as it has
been reformed since the Second Vatican Council.

In the history of Christian spirituality, the art and
labors of prayer are incarnated in the life stories of flesh-
and-blood Christians as they encounter both Word and
world. As such, this book has been a labor of love. Its
birth has been midwifed by many whose names are held
in prayer. However, I must express my thanks to Michael
Walsh, Jr., and Denise Douglas, both of whom urged me
to complete the project; to Carl Koch, FSC, and the
staff of Saint Mary's Press; to Curtis Bryant, SJ, Bradford
Brodeur, and the Community of Saint Luke for helping
me to carve these words as "primary speech" from human
beings before a merciful and passionate God. I hope that
this book will contribute to the life of prayer for all
those who hunger and thirst for Christ Jesus.

Introduction

Praying at Dawn and Dusk

Some moments of the day speak of and symbolize deeper experiences of time and life. Two special times are dawn and dusk. The rising of the sun evokes images of birth or new life. With the sun's setting at dusk emerge images of death and dying. In religious discourse, dawn and dusk became times when people adored and thanked God, and gave praise and expressed their need for forgiveness.

In Christ's death and resurrection, time is given new meaning. The dusk of the day reminds us of the darkness of sin and death from which Christians have been freed by the Messiah, God-with-us. For the believer, the dawn of a new day renews faith in creation and covenant, stirs a longing for God, and strengthens hope in the resurrection of Jesus.

Many religions encourage or mandate periods of prayer at dawn and at dusk. Consistent with Jewish practice, the early church used both dawn and dusk as privileged moments of communal prayer. Eventually prayers at morning and evening grew into the more complete liturgy of the hours. But use of the hours as a celebration of the church's worship by laypeople declined over the centuries. For lay Christians, devotional prayers supplanted the recitation of the hours.

In the spirit of liturgical renewal resulting from Vatican Council II, many Christians have sought to pray in harmony with the universal church. However, they find the entire liturgy of the hours complicated, difficult to understand, and too demanding of their time. Although *Prayers for Dawn and Dusk* does not attempt to be a short version of the liturgy of the hours, some elements of the Catholic church's official prayer are contained in it. Each morning and evening prayer begins with an invocation and then offers a psalm for prayer, a time for intercession or praise, and a closing. Sundays and major feasts offer a morning prayer and two evening prayers. The first evening prayer is to be celebrated the evening before that particular Sunday or feast.

The parts of the book are arranged by liturgical season, namely Advent, Christmas with its major feasts, Ordinary Time, Lent, the Sacred Triduum, and Easter with its feasts. The last part offers prayers for various needs and occasions.

Praying the Psalms is central to using *Prayers for Dawn and Dusk*. In the Book of Psalms, we find brought together the deepest emotions of the Jews and their religious beliefs. The Psalms were and still are the everyday prayer of Jews. These prayers arose out of many specific historical contexts, most of which we know little about.

Praying with the Psalms

Reading the Psalms or listening to them being sung is like listening in on the intense, honest, emotional conversation of lovers who are not afraid to be themselves with each other, even when being themselves does not present a lovely, pleasant picture. These hymns express praise, thanks, wonder, joy, struggle, guilt, doubts, fears, anger, even hatred. The psalmists share everything about their lives and experiences with their God.

In his book *Praying the Psalms*, Walter Brueggemann describes ways in which the honesty and passion of the Psalms may be better understood:

> The Psalms thus propose to speak about human experience in an honest, freeing way. This is in contrast to much human speech and conduct which is in fact a cover-up. . . .
>
> . . . The speech of the Psalms is abrasive, revolutionary, and dangerous. It announces . . . that our common experience is not one of well-being and equilibrium, but a churning, disruptive experience of dislocation and relocation.
>
> . . . There is no mediation to "clean up," censor, or filter what is going on. . . . There are no secrets hid from God, so there likely is less self-deception at work in these prayers. . . .
>
> The practice of concreteness and candor, of anger and hope, . . . prepare us for the most striking and problematic element of Jewish prayer, the *readiness to seek vengeance.*

*. . . The yearning for vengeance is here, among us
and within us* and with power. It is not only *there* in
the Psalms but it is *here* in the human heart and the
human community. . . . The Psalms do "tell it like
it is" with us. . . .

It is important to recognize that these verbal
assaults of imagination and hyperbole are *verbal*.
They speak wishes and prayers. But the speaker
doesn't *do* anything beyond speak. . . .

. . . This full rage and bitterness is *yielded to
God's wisdom and providential care*. (Pp. 19–20,
59–62, 68–71).

The Psalms express what is deepest and most honest in
the human heart, and they always end hopefully because
the psalmists trusted that God would act faithfully and
justly on their behalf.

As you pray the Psalms in this book, allow yourself
to feel what the psalmists say. When a psalm laments
captivity, lament your captivity not to the Babylonians
but to hurtful habits or harmful relationships. When a
psalm praises God for the seas and sky, praise God for
the nature around you. See the seas and sky as symbols
of all God's creation, all that nourishes your body, spirit,
and mind. And when a psalm pleads that God wreck
vengeance on enemies, let your own anger and desire for
vengeance be purged as you express yourself using the
psalmists' words. The spirit of praying the Psalms must
be a spirit of absolute honesty with a loving God who
knows our hearts and minds.

**Using
the Prayers**

Whether you use these prayers alone or with a group, try
to create a prayerful mood with candles, an open Bible,
or a crucifix. If a quiet place is not available, know that
a loving God is present everywhere.

The use of first-person plural in the prayers is
meant to remind individuals that all our praying takes
place as members of the corporate Body of Christ. The
intercessions and praise lists are each introduced by an
italicized phrase, which is the response called for by the
ellipses in each prayer that follows.

The prayers in this book may be freely adapted to meet your needs. For instance, add a hymn at the start or the end of a prayer. Other suggestions follow.

Begin by silently recalling God's presence. If you feel restless or rushed, spend some moments simply relaxing your body, letting go of all the tensions of the day, all the time demands, all your projects. Breathe deeply and slowly. A period of meditative breathing in God's presence is a prayer of simple attention. If you find it helpful, repeat a short prayer-phrase in harmony with your breathing. For example, "You are present, Holy Friend." When you are present to God, engage in the rest of the prayer, starting with a recitation of the opening prayer of adoration or thanksgiving.

Pray each of the sections carefully, letting the meaning of the words take form for you. Each word and phrase is an offering to God. Give your offering deliberately. Pause in silence between each section.

At the end of the psalm, the ancient prayer Glory Be may be added. You might wish to use this inclusive-language paraphrase of the Glory Be: *Glory be to God our creator, to Jesus the Christ, and to the Holy Spirit who dwells in our midst, both now and forever. Amen.* As time permits, meditate on the meaning of the psalm as it applies to you, your family, or your local community.

Some people enjoy reading selected passages from the Bible or other worthwhile literature after praying the psalm. For those following the liturgical cycle of biblical texts, the readings for the day might serve as a focus for reflection.

The sections Praise (morning) and Intercessions (evening) provide an opportunity for you to add prayers of praise and petition particularly important or relevant for you. In the morning, consider problems that might confront you during the day or people who need your attention. In the evening, pause to do an examination of conscience. Reflect on how God acted in your life during the day, how you responded, and perhaps how you would like to be more Christlike the next day. Before the closing prayer, recitation of the Lord's Prayer may be included.

Praying at dawn begins the day with an offering to God of our attention, work, relationships, and hopes. Ending the day with prayer allows us to review what we have done and who we have been, and to offer our day once again to a loving God.

Advent and O Antiphons

Advent Sundays

Thanksgiving

All praise and thanks to you,
God of the starry night,
for the light of Christ,
which blazes forth and scatters our darkness.
In this holy season,
your people turn their faces
to the coming of your justice and peace.
Amid the approaching shades and chill of earth,
we await the return of the Savior
whose coming is our hope and your promise.
Your power is kindled as evening falls
so that we may not be tempted to despair.
All praise and thanks be yours
through Christ and the Holy Spirit
forever and ever. Amen.

Psalm 141

Yahweh, I am calling. Hasten to me;
hear me—I am calling to you.
My prayers rise like incense,
my hands like the evening sacrifice.
Yahweh, set a guard at my mouth,
a watch at the door of my lips.
Do not let my heart be compelled to wrong doing,
to share in the deeds of the evildoers.
No, I will not taste their delights.
A just person may strike me in reproof—
it is a kindness;
such a rebuke is oil on my head!
My prayer is ever against the deeds of evildoers.
To you, Yahweh, I turn my eyes.
In you I take shelter—
do not hand me over to death.

Keep me out of traps that are set for me,
from the bait laid for me by evil ones.

(Vv. 1–5,8–9)

Although darkness falls, we hope. In confidence we
place our needs before the Source of All Peace, as we
pray: *May your mercy rest on us.*
- For the church, that we may be faithful watchers for
  the coming of the Savior, let us pray . . .
- For all those who lead us in faith and all those who
  move us to deeds of justice and peace, let us pray . . .
- For our community, that we may welcome the
  strangers, the aliens, and the poor people as the signs
  of God's presence in our midst, let us pray . . .
- For the sick people, the lonely people, and those who
  are caught in the grip of sin's bitterness and chill, let
  us pray . . .
- For those who have died, that heaven's glory may
  now be the reward of their hope, let us pray . . .
- (Other spontaneous prayers of intercession or contrition, or an examination of conscience) . . .

O God of might and power, we look to the coming of
your reign. Let not the darkness of despair rule over our
minds and hearts. Let the bright promise of Christ's
coming again enkindle in us the fire of your love. We
ask this through Christ our savior. Amen.

Intercessions

Closing

MORNING

Adoration

God of the everlasting dawn,
we give you heartfelt praise and glory.
A people that walked in darkness
live now in the hope of your eternal light
of justice and peace.
The brightness of the Risen Christ
is the pledge of your providence.
In this holy season,
we look again
to the coming of the Victorious One,
who has forever banished
the sting of death.

All glory and honor be yours
with Christ and the Holy Spirit
forever and ever. Amen.

Psalm 63

O God, you are my God whom I eagerly seek;
for you my flesh longs and my soul thirsts
like the earth, parched, lifeless, and without water.
I have gazed toward you in the sanctuary
to see your power and your glory.
For your love is better than life;
my lips shall glorify you.
Thus will I praise you while I live;
lifting up my hands, I will call upon your name.
As with the riches of a banquet shall my soul be filled,
and with exultant lips my mouth shall praise you.
On my bed I will remember you,
and through the night watches I will meditate on you:
because you are my help,
and in the shadow of your wings I shout for joy.
My soul clings to you;
your right hand upholds me.

(Vv. 1–8)

Praise

As the peace of heaven dawns upon us, we raise our
voices in praise: *Blessings on our faithful God.*
- We give praise to God, who always draws close to us,
  as we pray . . .
- We honor our creator, whose promises are ever un-
  folding among us, as we pray . . .
- We bless the ever-living God, whose Christ has won
  salvation for us, as we pray . . .
- We rejoice at the coming of the justice and mercy of
  God, as we pray . . .
- (Other spontaneous prayers of petition or praise) . . .

Closing

God, whose advent is ever before our eyes, our hearts
rejoice even amid the threat of evil. In Christ, you
have given us the hope of your reign. May your spirit
strengthen the frailty of our hearts. We ask this through
Christ our savior. Amen.

Thanksgiving

We give you thanks, ever-present God,
and we offer to you
our evening sacrifice of praise.
As darkness falls upon us,
we rejoice that you have given us
the light of Christ to guide us
through this life to eternal joy.
The promise of Christ to return to us
with the fullness of your love
is the hope that makes our hearts yearn
for your presence.
With great joy, we await the return of Jesus
and look to that day
when poor and downtrodden people
shall feast on your holy mountain.
All praise and thanks be yours
through Christ and the Holy Spirit
forever and ever. Amen.

Psalm 115

Not to us, Yahweh, not to us,
but to you alone give the glory
because of your love and your faithfulness.
Or some nations will say: "Where is their God?"
But our God is in the heavens
doing whatever God wills.
Their idols are silver and gold,
the work of human hands.
They have mouths but cannot speak;
they have eyes but cannot see;
they have ears but cannot hear;
they have nostrils but cannot smell.
With their hands they cannot feel;
with their feet they cannot walk.
No sound comes from their throats.
Those who make them will be like them
and so will all who trust in them.
The dead shall not praise Yahweh,
nor those who go down into the silence.

But we who live bless Yahweh
now and forever. Amen.

(Vv. 1–8,17–18)

Intercessions

As the earth longs for the reign of God, we offer all the needs of God's people to Jesus our brother, as we pray: *Visit us and hear our prayer.*

- For Christians everywhere, that we may thirst for the fullness of God's justice and peace, let us pray . . .
- For the nations, that the mercy of God may be the cornerstone of every law and custom, let us pray . . .
- For our community, that this season may find us growing more deeply into the love of Jesus Christ, let us pray . . .
- For our community, that the advent of Jesus' coming may move us to be advocates for God's poor and helpless people, let us pray . . .
- For the faithful departed, that they may now rest in light, happiness, and peace, let us pray . . .
- (Other spontaneous prayers of intercession or contrition, or an examination of conscience) . . .

Closing

O God of all kindness, we await with hope the coming of your reign. May hope dwell in our minds and hearts. Let the bright promise of Christ's coming kindle in us the fire of your love. We ask this through Christ our savior. Amen.

Advent Mondays
Until 17 December

Adoration

Bright Dawn of All Wisdom,
we adore you and bless your name.
Wintry earth
looks to the warmth of your love
and the fullness of your peace
as the promise of a new and eternal springtime.
As daylight scatters the shades of night,
we yearn for that final season
when all peoples will come
to the glory of Zion.
All honor and blessing be yours
through Christ and the Holy Spirit
forever and ever. Amen.

Psalm 42

Like the deer that yearns
for running streams,
so my soul is yearning
for you, my God.
My soul is thirsting for God, the living God.
When can I enter to see the face of God?
My tears have become my food night and day,
and I hear it said all day long:
"Where is your God?"
I will remember all these things
as I pour out my soul:
how I would lead the joyous procession
into the house of God,
with cries of gladness and thanksgiving,
the multitude wildly happy.
Why are you so sad, my soul?
Why sigh within me?

Hope in God;
for I will yet praise my savior and my God.

(Vv. 1–5)

Praise As daylight dawns, we offer praise to God, who is always faithful, as we pray: *Honor to the Font of Life.*
- Our chilled hearts thrill at the coming of our God, and we pray . . .
- Our bruised bones dance at the dawn of God's justice, and we pray . . .
- Broken earth is bathed in the glory of hope, and we pray . . .
- All peoples look to the day of God's reign, and we pray . . .
- (Other spontaneous prayers of petition or praise) . . .

Closing Gracious God, we await the advent of your final glory when every tear shall be wiped away and hungry people shall have their fill. Grant us the Spirit of all hope that the darkness of war and oppression may give way to the fullness of the victory of Christ. We ask this through Christ our holy friend. Amen.

EVENING

Thanksgiving God, who enflames the hearts
of those chained in darkness,
the shades of evening fall upon us,
and we give you thanks
for the blessings of this day.
During this night,
we acclaim Christ as the pillar of fire
that leads us onward to dawn's liberty.
As we await the coming of Christ in glory,
we are filled with the Spirit of hope,
who is our advocate and our guide.
All praise and thanks be yours
through Christ and the Holy Spirit
forever and ever. Amen.

My heart overflows with a goodly theme;
I address my verses to the king;
my tongue is like the pen of a ready scribe.
You are the fairest of all;
grace is poured upon your lips;
thus God has blessed you forever.
Gird your sword upon your side, O mighty one,
clothe yourself with glory and majesty!
Hear, O daughter, consider, and turn your ear;
forget your people and your ancestor's home.
The king will desire your beauty.
The people of Tyre are here with gifts,
the richest of the people seeking your favor.
The place of your ancestors your children shall have;
you will make them rulers through all the earth.
I will cause your name to be celebrated in all
　　　generations;
therefore the peoples will praise you forever and ever.
(Vv. 1–3,10–12,16–17)

Psalm 45

Yearning for Christ's coming, we offer the needs of God's people, as we pray: *Come to us, lest we forget.*
- For the church in the world, that we may be faithful to the coming of the Christ, let us pray . . .
- For all the nations, that the peace and justice of Christ may heal divisions, let us pray . . .
- For our community, in thanksgiving for the generosity of all those who make our life possible, let us pray . . .
- For poor and lowly people, that the God of fidelity may move us to a more generous service of the dispossessed, let us pray . . .
- For those who have died, that their journey into joy may be marked with all peace, let us pray . . .
- (Other spontaneous prayers of intercession or contrition, or an examination of conscience) . . .

Intercessions

Faithful God, we await the advent of your final glory when every tear shall be wiped away and hungry people shall have their fill. Grant us the Spirit of all hope that the darkness of war and oppression may give way to the fullness of the victory of Christ. We ask this through Christ our peace. Amen.

Closing

Advent Tuesdays Until 17 December

MORNING

Adoration

Loving God,
we give you praise
as the bright sun of your justice
continually scatters the clouds of sin and despair.
From the broken shards of David's line,
you brought forth in Christ
a new royalty and a priesthood for all peoples.
We, your people, look to that day
when Christ shall crown all creation
with the final blessings of the Resurrection,
and thereby bring all things
to a new heaven and a new earth.
All honor and blessing be yours
through Christ and the Holy Spirit
forever and ever. Amen.

Psalm 43

Do me justice, O God, and plead my cause
against a faithless people;
from the deceitful and unjust, rescue me.
For you, O God, are my stronghold.
Why do you keep me so far away?
Why must I go about in mourning,
oppressed by the enemy?
Send forth your light and your truth—
they shall guide me;
let them bring me to your holy mountain,
to your dwelling place.
Then will I go in to the altar of God,
the God of my delight and joy;
then will I praise you with the harp,
O God, my God!

Why are you so downcast, O my soul?
Why do you sigh within me?
Put your hope in God, for I shall again be thankful
in the presence of my savior and my God.

Longing for the coming of our Savior, we give praise to **Praise**
God, as we pray: *God of glory, we bless your name.*
- All creation rejoices at the bright promise of immortality, and we pray . . .
- In the hope of God's justice, we pray . . .
- For the promise of glory from the coming of God's reign, we pray . . .
- To our faithful God, we pray . . .
- (Other spontaneous prayers of petition or praise) . . .

God of light, we rejoice at the advent of the Christ, **Closing**
when Israel and all creation shall come to freedom from
the slavery of sin and death. Grant us the gift of your
Spirit so that we may ever proclaim your covenant of
love. We ask this through Christ, who teaches us how to
love. Amen.

EVENING

Almighty and tender God, **Thanksgiving**
we give you thanks and praise
for the gift of Christ,
who is forever the lamp of your holy temple.
Together with the children of Sarah and Abraham,
we look forward to the coming of your light,
which will destroy forever the terror of night.
As daylight fails,
we gather in gratitude and repentance,
hoping for the coming of your eternal dawn.
The advent of Christ is the cause of our joy
and the hope that dispels our despair.
All praise and thanks be yours
through Christ and the Holy Spirit
forever and ever. Amen.

Psalm 62 | For God alone my soul waits.
My help comes from God,
who alone is my rock, my stronghold, my fortress:
I stand firm.
How long will you all attack me
to break me down
as though I were a tottering wall
or a sagging fence?
Their plan is only to destroy.
They take pleasure in lies.
With their mouths they utter blessing,
but in their hearts they curse.
For God alone my soul waits;
for my hope comes from God,
who alone is my rock, my stronghold, my fortress.
I stand firm.
In God is my salvation and glory,
the rock of my strength.

(Vv. 1–7)

Intercessions | As the shades of evening descend upon the earth, in
hope we offer our needs to our gracious God, and we
pray: *Come to us and hear our prayer.*
- For all God's people, that we may be faithful to the
  covenant, let us pray . . .
- For all nations, that the covenant may be the vision
  of hope for all, let us pray . . .
- For our community, for those who serve us and for
  those whom we serve, let us pray . . .
- For those who dwell in the shadow of death, that the
  light of Christ may set them free, let us pray . . .
- For those who have passed to the celestial lights of
  God's peace, let us pray . . .
- (Other spontaneous prayers of intercession or contri-
  tion, or an examination of conscience) . . .

Closing | God of light, we rejoice at the advent of Christ, when
Israel and all creation shall come to freedom from the
slavery of sin and death. Grant us the gift of your Spirit
so that we may ever proclaim your covenant of love. We
ask this through Christ, who is love. Amen.

Advent Wednesdays
Until 17 December

Adoration

Blessed are you, God of truth,
for in the fullness of time
you sent forth your Word
as the salvation of all.
Jesus is the dawn that scatters the night,
the bright promise of immortality.
In these days,
we look forward to that season
wherein your justice and peace
shall flower in the desert of the earth.
When Christ comes again,
you will gather the nations
under the shelter of your wings,
and death shall sting no longer.
All honor and glory be yours
through Christ and the Holy Spirit
forever and ever. Amen.

Psalm 77

I cried aloud to you, O God;
I cried, and you heard me.
In the day of my distress I sought you, Yahweh,
and by night I stretched out my hands in prayer.
I lay sweating and nothing would cool me;
I refused all comfort.
When I remembered you, I groaned;
as I pondered, darkness came over my spirit.
Yahweh, will you reject us forever
and never again show us your favor?
Has your unfailing love now failed us completely?
Will your promise be unfulfilled?
Have you forgotten how to be gracious?

Have you withheld your compassion in anger?
Has your right hand changed?
Is the arm of the Most High powerless?
But then I remember your deeds;
I recall your wonders in times gone by.
I meditate upon your works
and ponder all that you have done.

(Vv. 1–3,7–12)

Praise

As the light bids us to the tasks of yet another day, we acclaim our God, who beckons us to the task of peace, as we pray: *Blessings on the Holy One.*
- We raise our voices and glorify God, as we pray . . .
- Our hearts rejoice at the dawn of justice, as we pray . . .
- Parched earth leaps at the voice of the God of love, as we pray . . .
- We look to God as the font of all blessings, as we pray . . .
- (Other spontaneous prayers of petition or praise) . . .

Closing

God, we give you thanks for the gift of salvation, and we look forward to the fullness of your love. Through the power of the Holy Spirit, keep us vigilant for the coming of Christ again. We ask this through Christ our savior. Amen.

EVENING

Thanksgiving

God of all goodness,
we give you thanks and praise as daylight fades.
Night approaches,
yet our hearts are not dimmed,
for the lamp of your love
burns brightly in our midst.
In Christ, all the earth has a new hope
that prevents the threat of despair
from brooding in our lives.
We yearn for the coming of Jesus the Christ,
when darkness is overcome by your everlasting glory.

All praise and thanks be yours
through Christ and the Holy Spirit
forever and ever. Amen.

Psalm 85

Yahweh, you have favored your land
and restored the well-being of Israel;
you have forgiven the guilt of your people
and covered all their sins.
You set aside all your rage;
you calmed the heat of your anger.
Restore us now, God, our Savior!
Put an end to your displeasure with us.
Your salvation is near for those who fear you,
and your glory will dwell in our land.
Love and faithfulness have met;
justice and peace have embraced.
Faithfulness shall spring from the earth
and justice look down from heaven.
Justice shall march before you,
and peace shall follow your steps.

(Vv. 1–4,9–11,13)

Intercessions | We look to the coming of the Christ and the fulfillment of our every desire. In that spirit, we offer our needs to God, as we pray: *May your peace descend upon us.*

- For all Christians, that we may be vigilant for the coming of the Christ, let us pray . . .
- For those who lead us in the faith and in government, that they may be strengthened to minister in the spirit of humility, let us pray . . .
- For our community, that this holy season may find us growing into unity of mind and heart, let us pray . . .
- For all those who suffer from the ravages of war and oppression, that the liberty of God's love may set them free, let us pray . . .
- For all those who have passed from this life, that the peace of Christ may be their inheritance, let us pray . . .
- (Other spontaneous prayers of intercession or contrition, or an examination of conscience) . . .

Closing | God, we give you thanks for the gift of salvation, and we look forward to the fullness of your love. Through the power of the Holy Spirit, keep us vigilant for the coming of Christ again. We ask this through Christ our redeemer. Amen.

Advent Thursdays
Until 17 December

Blessed are you, God of glory,
for gathering us into your marvelous light.
As daylight bursts upon us,
we adore you as the only God,
the source of all life.
In Christ, you have chosen us
as your pilgrim people who journey yet
toward the fullness of your love.
In this holy season, our faces are set
toward the vision of your justice and peace,
and the hearts of believers are filled with hope.
All honor and blessing be yours
through Christ and the Holy Spirit
forever and ever. Amen.

Adoration

Hear me, O Shepherd of Israel!
You who guide Joseph like a flock.
Enthroned on the cherubs, shine out
on Ephraim, Benjamin, and Manasseh.
Rouse your power and come to save us!
Restore us, Yahweh.
We will be secure when you smile upon us.
How long will you be angry, Yahweh,
while your people pray?
O Yahweh, please return!
Look down from heaven and see this vine.
Nurture and guard what your hand has planted.
Safeguard those you have chosen,
those you have made strong.
Never again will we turn away from you;
we shall call on your holy name with a renewed spirit.

Psalm 80

Restore us, Yahweh Sabaoth;
let your face smile on us—
then we will be safe.

(Vv. 1–4,14–15,17–19)

Praise

As we look to the coming of the Savior, we praise our mighty and tender God by praying: *Holy God, we praise your name.*

- Our hearts give homage to the God of light, as we pray . . .
- We glorify the God who is the peace of every nation, as we pray . . .
- As a pilgrim people we bless Christ, who scatters all darkness, as we pray . . .
- We bless God, who hears the cries of poor people, as we pray . . .
- (Other spontaneous prayers of petition or praise) . . .

Closing

God of all life, we give you praise this day for the coming of your reign. Grant us the gift of the Spirit so that we may be filled with hope on this, our earthly pilgrimage. We ask this through Christ our shepherd. Amen.

EVENING

Thanksgiving

God-with-us,
we give you praise and thanks
for the blessings of this holy season.
In Christ, we have been given a new light
that forever shatters the power of evil.
As night falls upon us,
we acclaim Jesus as the hope of all the ages
and the cause of our joy.
The Risen One enlightens the shades of evening
and leads us to the day of your peace and reconciliation.
All praise and thanks be yours
through Christ and the Holy Spirit
forever and ever. Amen.

O God, with your judgment and with your justice,
endow the leaders.
They shall govern your people with justice
and your afflicted ones with righteousness.
The mountains will bring peace for the people,
and the hills justice.
They shall defend the afflicted among the people,
save the children of the poor,
and crush the oppressor.
May they endure as long as the sun
and like the moon through all generations.
They shall be like rain coming down on the field,
like showers watering the earth.
Virtue shall flower in their days,
and world peace till the moon is no more.
May they rule from sea to sea,
and from the river to the ends of the earth.

(Vv. 1–8)

Psalm 72

As we come to the end of yet another day, we look
forward to a new dawn, and we offer this prayer: *May
your advent be our hope.*
- For the church, that all peoples may be gathered into
  the love of God, let us pray . . .
- For the nations, that hostilities between peoples and
  between nations may come to an end, let us pray . . .
- For our gathering in this holy place, that we may be
  deepened in our conversion to Jesus, let us pray . . .
- For all those who are bereft of hope, that the longing
  of this Advent may be a sign of Christian companionship with all those who suffer, let us pray . . .
- For the dead, that the peace of heaven may now be
  theirs, let us pray . . .
- (Other spontaneous prayers of intercession or contrition, or an examination of conscience) . . .

Intercessions

God of all life, we give you praise this day for the coming
of your reign. Grant us the gift of the Spirit so that we
may be filled with hope on this, our earthly pilgrimage.
We ask this through Christ our shepherd. Amen.

Closing

Advent Fridays
Until 17 December

MORNING

Adoration

Eternal God, we adore you
and offer our morning praise.
This day we recall
that tender gift of your love
poured out for us on Calvary's height.
In the blood of the Lamb,
the darkness of evil has been vanquished,
and you won for yourself a grateful people.
In these days, we set our faces
toward the new and eternal Jerusalem,
and look for that day
when mercy and faithfulness shall embrace.
As we thirst for you,
we give you all honor and adoration
through Christ and the Holy Spirit
forever and ever. Amen.

Psalm 51

In your goodness, O God, have mercy on me;
with gentleness wipe away my faults.
Cleanse me of guilt;
free me from my sins.
My faults are always before me;
my sins haunt my mind.
As you know I was born in guilt,
from conception a sinner at heart.
But you love true sincerity,
so you teach me the depths of wisdom.
Until I am clean, bathe me with hyssop;
wash me until I am whiter than snow.
Create a pure heart in me, O my God;
renew me with a steadfast spirit.

Sacrifices give you no pleasure;
if I offered a holocaust, you would refuse it.
My sacrifice is this broken spirit.
You will not disdain a contrite and humbled heart.
Graciously show your favor to Zion;
rebuild the walls of Jerusalem.

(Vv. 1–3,5–7,10,16–18)

As our souls awaken to the music of this day, we bless our God, who has saved us by the cross of Christ, as we pray: *God of love, be blessed.*

Praise

- We adore our God, who beckons us to the final victory of Christ, as we pray . . .
- We are filled with praise at the coming joys of God, as we pray . . .
- We stand in awe of the merciful love of God, as we pray . . .
- We are filled with wonder at the salvation that is ours, as we pray . . .
- (Other spontaneous prayers of petition or praise) . . .

Merciful God, this day we are filled with gratitude for the salvation that is ours. When Jesus embraced our frail humanity, wounded earth was made whole. Keep us faithful to the cross until Christ comes again. We ask this through Christ, God-with-us. Amen.

Closing

EVENING

Holy and Immortal One,
tonight we give you thanks and praise.
As we journey through this Advent season,
we look to the fullness of your justice,
which will dispel the dark night of evil.
In the blood of Jesus,
your loving reign has begun,
and all the earth is filled with hope.
We acclaim you,
for the winter night
of the Prince of Darkness
has been conquered,

Thanksgiving

and the lamp of our joy
has blazed forth in our midst.
All praise and thanks be yours
through Christ and the Holy Spirit
forever and ever. Amen.

Psalm 121

I lift my eyes to the mountains.
Where is help to come from?
My help comes from Yahweh,
who made heaven and earth.
Yahweh does not let our footsteps slip!
Our guard does not sleep!
The guardian of Israel
does not slumber or sleep.
Yahweh guards you, shades you.
With Yahweh at your right hand
the sun cannot harm you by day
nor the moon at night.
Yahweh guards you from harm,
protects your lives;
Yahweh watches over your coming and going,
now and for always.

Intercessions

Grateful for the salvation that is ours in Christ, we offer
our needs to the Creator, as we pray: *God, anoint us with
your love.*

- For all the people of God, that we may be faithful
  witnesses to the Lamb, let us pray . . .
- For those who minister to us in the faith, that they
  may know the gifts of wisdom and compassion, let us
  pray . . .
- For our community, that our witness of love and kindness may be the leaven of goodness, let us pray . . .
- For downtrodden people and those most lowly among
  us, that we may be moved to a more generous service
  of them, let us pray . . .
- For all those who have gone beyond the veil of death,
  that God may grant them a peace beyond all understanding, let us pray . . .
- (Other spontaneous prayers of intercession or contrition, or an examination of conscience) . . .

Merciful God, this day we are filled with gratitude for the salvation that is ours. When Jesus embraced our frail humanity, wounded earth was made whole. Keep us faithful to the cross until Christ comes again. We ask this through Christ our redeemer. Amen.

Closing

Advent Saturdays
Until 17 December

MORNING

Adoration
God of all creation,
in the beginning,
your spirit hovered over the waters of chaos
and brought all life into being.
In the fullness of time,
your spirit hovered over Mary,
and the Promised One was born in our flesh.
This same spirit clothes your people
so that the presence of Jesus
may be born each day for all the world.
In this Advent pilgrimage,
we look to the final dawn of the Christ among us
when a new heaven and a new earth
will spring from the womb of your goodness.
As daylight dawns among us,
we give you praise and glory
through Christ and the Holy Spirit
forever and ever. Amen.

Psalm 8
O God, our God,
how glorious is your name over all the earth!
Your glory is praised in the heavens.
Out of the mouths of children and babes
you have fashioned praise because of your foes,
to silence the enemy and the rebellious.
When I look at your heavens, the work of your hands,
the moon and the stars which you created—
who are we that you should be mindful of us,
that you should care for us?
You have made us little less than the gods
and crowned us with glory and honor.

You have given us rule over the works of your hands,
putting all things under our feet:
all sheep and oxen,
yes, and the beasts of the field;
the birds of the air, the fishes of the sea,
and whatever swims the paths of the seas.
God, our God,
how glorious is your name over all the earth!

Praise

In the spirit of Holy Mary, faithful to her Son, we praise
our loving God, who is always beckoning us onward, as
we pray: *All the earth, give praise to God.*
• We bless our God, who calls us to deeds of justice, as
we pray . . .
• We adore God who is the blessing of mercy for us all,
as we pray . . .
• We give thanks to God for the vision of true peace, as
we pray . . .
• We are grateful to God for the presence of the Word
made flesh, as we pray . . .
• (Other spontaneous prayers of petition or praise) . . .

Closing

Merciful God, whose providence for us in Christ satisfies
the yearning of every race and people, we give you
thanks for the blessings you bestow upon us as we look
for the coming of your reign. As you made the Virgin
Mother the very image of true discipleship through the
power of the Holy Spirit, make us faithful witnesses to
Christ Jesus. We ask this through Christ our brother.
Amen.

Advent from 17 to 24 December: The O Antiphons

MORNING

Adoration

O eternal and provident God,
we give you praise and adoration
as daylight comes upon us.
In the fullness of time,
you breathed forth your Spirit upon Mary,
and the Word became flesh in her womb.
Jesus became for all the earth
the root of Jesse,
the king of the nations,
and the brilliant sun of justice.
Wintry earth is warmed by the radiance
that has dawned in Christ,
and the hopes and dreams of longing people
have come to fulfillment.
All honor and blessing be yours
through Christ and the Holy Spirit
forever and ever. Amen.

Psalm 47

All you peoples, clap your hands;
raise a joyful shout to God.
For the Most High is awesome,
glorious over all the earth.
God subdues peoples under us
and puts nations at our feet.
The God of Love chooses for us our inheritance,
the pride of Jacob.
God has ascended amid shouts of joy and trumpet peals.
Sing praise to God, sing praise,
for God is the Most High over all the earth.

Sing hymns of praise.
God rules over all the nations;
God sits upon the holy throne.
The nobles of the nations are gathered
with the people of the God of Abraham and Sarah.
For the guardians of the earth are God's.
Over all is God exalted.

As we look to the coming celebration of the birth of **Praise**
Christ Jesus, we acclaim our God, who in Christ did not
shrink from our humanity, and we pray: *Praise be to you,*
God of love.
- In joy we celebrate the birth of our salvation, as we
  pray . . .
- In love we honor the intimacy of God, which has
  redeemed our poverty, as we pray . . .
- In peace we are filled with awe at the coming cele-
  bration of the birth of Christ, as we pray . . .
- In humility we acclaim the goodness of God in the
  gift of Emmanuel—God-with-us—as we pray . . .
- (Other spontaneous prayers of petition or praise) . . .

Gracious God, faithful to promises, we rejoice at the **Closing**
coming celebration of the birth of the Messiah. By the
power of your Holy Spirit, may we always bear the gifts
of justice and peace into our world. We ask this through
Christ, the bringer-of-peace. Amen.

EVENING

O merciful and tender God, **Thanksgiving**
we offer you thanks and praise
for the gift of the Christ,
who forever dwells within our midst.
Abraham and Sarah rejoiced to see his day.
David yearned for his presence.
Now we understand that this Christ
is the key of salvation, the leader of the new Israel,
the Emmanuel who has pitched your tent among us.
As evening falls,
we are filled with the spirit of gratitude
for your wondrous works within our lives.

All praise and thanks be yours
through Christ and the Holy Spirit
forever and ever. Amen.

Psalm 130

Out of the depths I cry to you, O God.
God, hear my voice!
Let your ears be attentive
to my cry for mercy.
If you, O God, mark our guilt,
who can stand?
But with you is forgiveness;
and for this we revere you.
I trust in you, O God,
my soul trusts in your word.
My soul waits for you, O God.
More than sentinels wait for the dawn,
let Israel wait for you.
For with you is faithful love
and plentiful redemption.
You will redeem Israel
from all their iniquities.

Intercessions

Despite the coming of darkness, our hope is not dimmed.
Now we offer the needs of all the earth to our God, who
has not abandoned us but embraces us in Christ, as we
pray: *May our lives sing forth your love.*
- For all Christians, that we may forever bear witness to
  the Emmanuel who is the pledge of the world's salvation, let us pray . . .
- For all the nations, that the birth of the Christ in our
  human poverty may move us to deeds of justice and
  peace, let us pray . . .
- For our community, that the approaching celebration
  of the birth of Jesus may find us bound more closely
  in love and compassion, let us pray . . .
- For those who dwell in loneliness, that they may
  know the freedom of the God whose touch heals
  human despair, let us pray . . .

- For those who have been guided by the radiance of Wisdom beyond this life, that they may know the peace of heaven's nativity, let us pray . . .
- (Other spontaneous prayers of intercession or contrition, or an examination of conscience) . . .

Gracious God, faithful to promises, we rejoice at the coming celebration of the birth of the Messiah. By the power of your Holy Spirit, may we always act with justice and peace in our weary world. We ask this through Christ, the bringer-of-peace. Amen.

Closing

Christmas

Christmas, Its Octave and the Sundays of the Season

Adoration

All honor, praise, and glory be yours, gracious God,
for the eternal dawn that has come upon us.
Today our hearts rejoice
for the coming of your Son into the world.
When Jesus took our flesh in the womb of Mary,
the bright promise of the ages was fulfilled
and the power of death trembled in fear.
Jesus came to us in humility
and did not shrink to touch
the depths of our humanity.
Worshipped by shepherds, Jesus was proclaimed
as the salvation of poor and lowly people.
Be praised, O God, in every season
for the wonder of your revelation in our midst.
Be praised through the newborn babe
and the Holy Spirit
forever and ever. Amen.

Psalm 150

Alleluia!
Praise to you, Yahweh, in your sanctuary!
Praise to you in the firmament of your strength.
Praise you for your mighty deeds;
praise you for your sovereign majesty.
Praise to you, Yahweh, with the blast of the trumpet,
praise with lyre and harp.
Praise with timbrel and dance;
praise with strings and flute.
Praise to you, Yahweh, with resounding cymbals;
praise with clanging cymbals.

Let everything that has breath praise Yahweh.
Alleluia.

Today we acclaim our God, who has taken on our flesh
in Jesus, as we pray: *Honor and praise to you, our God.*
- We adore you, God, who assumed the frailty of our
  humanity, as we pray . . .
- We are filled with awe at the incarnation of you, our
  God, as we pray . . .
- Our bruised flesh thrills at the salvation and healing
  found in the birth of the Christ, as we pray . . .
- We acclaim the birth of Christ as the brilliant and
  final Sun of True Justice, as we pray . . .
- (Other spontaneous prayers of petition or praise) . . .

Praise

Faithful God, when the ancient curse of the Evil One
held your people in bondage, you did not abandon them
to death's sting but promised a redeemer. Today we
celebrate the birth of Christ in the flesh. Cradled by
Mary and Joseph, warmed by common beasts and straw,
adored by simple folk, this Christ is the cause of our joy.
Teach us always to proclaim the beauty of this holy birth
and bring us at last to the fullness of your peace. We ask
this through Christ our salvation. Amen.

Closing

**FIRST AND
SECOND
EVENING**

Ever-living God,
we give you thanks and praise this night
for the gift of this most sacred festival.
Your people walked in darkness
but not without the bright promise of your Christ.
Chained by ancient fears,
the nations looked with longing
for the coming of a savior
who would lead them to liberty and justice.
Dark earth yearned for the coming of a light
that would forever dispel
the mists of eternal night.

Thanksgiving

This night and always,
we proclaim the fulfillment of your promises
through the birth of Jesus our savior.
All thanks and praise be yours
through Christ and the Holy Spirit
forever and ever. Amen.

Psalm 110

"Sit at my right hand
until I make your enemies a footstool for your feet."
Yahweh, send forth your mighty scepter from Zion.
Rule in the midst of your enemies!
Your people will offer themselves freely
on the day you lead your host upon the holy mountains.
Like dew from the womb of the dawn
your youth will come to you.
Yahweh has sworn and will not retract:
"You are a priest forever
after the order of Melchizedek."
Yahweh is at your right hand
and will shatter rulers on the day of wrath.
Yahweh will execute judgment among the nations,
filling them with corpses,
scattering them over the earth.
Yahweh will drink from the brook by the way,
therefore strengthened and victorious!

Intercessions

Christ Jesus is the fulfillment of God's promises for every
human need. Let us offer our longings to the God of all
faithfulness, as we pray: *Keep us mindful of your love.*

- For all the church, that the mystery of this holy night
  may be our lamp as we journey toward the final dawn
  of justice and peace, let us pray . . .
- For all people, that the birth of our Savior may be
  a proclamation of a new dawn of freedom, let us
  pray . . .
- For our community, that the mystery of the Incarnation may be the message that we proclaim in deed
  and word, let us pray . . .
- For lowly and poor people, for all those who are
  humbled, that the spirit of this holy feast may be their
  courage and their strength, let us pray . . .

- For all those who have died, that through the new-born Christ they may come to the new birth of heaven's joy, let us pray . . .
- (Other spontaneous prayers of intercession or contrition, or an examination of conscience) . . .

Faithful God, when the ancient curse of the Evil One held your people in bondage, you did not abandon them to death's sting but promised a redeemer. Today we celebrate the birth of Christ in the flesh. Cradled by Mary and Joseph, warmed by common beasts and straw, adored by simple folk, this Christ is the cause of our joy. Teach us always to proclaim the beauty of this holy birth and bring us at last to the fullness of your peace. We ask this through Christ our peace. Amen.

Closing

Christmas Mondays, Wednesdays, and Fridays Outside the Octave

Adoration

Blessed may you be, God of all kindness,
for your salvation that has dawned in our midst.
In these days of celebration,
we remember the birth of Jesus
as the fulfillment of your bright promise of immortality.
We rejoice that Christ did not shrink
to assume our flesh in the womb of the Virgin Mary.
As daylight spreads before us,
we are consumed with love of your holy will.
Heaven and earth are wed,
and all creation gives you praise
through Christ and the Holy Spirit
forever and ever. Amen.

Psalm 148

Praise God from the heavens;
praise God in the heights;
praise God, all you angels;
praise God, all you heavenly hosts.
Praise God, sun and moon;
praise God, all you shining stars.
Praise God, you highest heavens,
and you waters above the heavens.
Let them praise the name of God,
who commanded and they were created.
God established them forever and ever
and gave a decree which shall not pass away.

Be this God praised by all the faithful ones,
by the children of Israel, the people close to God.
Alleluia.

(Vv. 1–6,14)

In this season, we rejoice that God in Christ has touched | **Praise**
our frail humanity, and we cry out: *Glory to God in the highest.*
- We acclaim you, mighty God, who is revealed for us in the Child, as we pray . . .
- With shepherds and sages we adore the Savior of the world, as we pray . . .
- With Joseph and Mary we ponder the love of God in our hearts, as we pray . . .
- With angels and all the hosts of heaven we cry out joyfully for the gift of our salvation, as we pray . . .
- (Other spontaneous prayers of petition or praise) . . .

God eternal, through your tender mercy the Word has | **Closing**
sprung forth, taking our flesh in the womb of Mary.
Breathe forth your spirit upon us that we may proclaim
the message of this Holy Child all the days of our lives.
We ask this through Christ our redeemer. Amen.

EVENING

Almighty and tender God, | **Thanksgiving**
we give you thanks and praise in every season.
The shades of evening fall upon us,
and yet our hearts are not dimmed.
In the silence of this holy night,
the brilliance of the Child
enlightens the darkness and scatters our fear.
In Jesus, born of our flesh,
you have revealed the power of your justice,
and your mercy for all the earth.
In the poverty of Christ's birth,
the richness of your providence is proclaimed.
For the greatness of this gift,
we give you thanks and praise this night
through the newborn Christ and the Holy Spirit
forever and ever. Amen.

Psalm 110

"Sit at my right hand
until I make your enemies a footstool for your feet."
Yahweh, send forth your mighty scepter from Zion.
Rule in the midst of your enemies!
Your people will offer themselves freely
on the day you lead your host upon the holy mountains.
Like dew from the womb of the dawn
your youth will come to you.
Yahweh has sworn and will not retract:
"You are a priest forever
after the order of Melchizedek."
Yahweh is at your right hand
and will shatter rulers on the day of wrath.
Yahweh will execute judgment among the nations,
filling them with corpses,
scattering them over the earth.
Yahweh will drink from the brook by the way,
therefore strengthened and victorious!

Intercessions

The Newborn Child is the fulfillment of the promises of
God. Let us present our needs to the God who yearns to
fill up what is lacking in our lives, as we pray: *Loving
God, hear our prayer.*

- For the church, that we may proclaim faithfully the
  message of the Prince of Peace, let us pray . . .
- For the nations, that the presence of Christ among us
  may bring to an end every hostility, let us pray . . .
- For our community, that this season may find us
  giving birth to the Word in the world, let us pray . . .
- For those for whom this season bears no joy or peace,
  that our Savior may move us to deeds of justice for
  them, let us pray . . .
- For those who have been born anew in heaven, that
  we may remain faithful to their memory and prayerful
  companionship, let us pray . . .
- (Other spontaneous prayers of intercession or contrition, or an examination of conscience) . . .

God eternal, from your tender mercy the Word has
sprung forth, taking our flesh in the womb of Mary.
Breathe forth your spirit upon us that we may proclaim
the message of this Holy Child all the days of our lives.
We ask this through Christ our hope. Amen.

Closing

Christmas Tuesdays, Thursdays, and Saturdays Outside the Octave

Adoration

All honor, praise, and glory be yours, Mighty God,
for the eternal dawn that has come upon us.
Today our hearts rejoice
for the coming of Christ into our world.
When Jesus took our flesh in the womb of Mary,
the bright promise of the ages was fulfilled
and death trembled.
Jesus came to us in humility
and did not shrink
to touch the depths of our humanity.
Worshipped by shepherds, Jesus was proclaimed
the salvation of poor and lowly people.
Be praised, God of love, for the wonder of your
    revelation.
Be praised through the Newborn Babe,
with the Holy Spirit
forever and ever. Amen.

Psalm 149

Sing to Yahweh a new song of praise
in the assembly of the faithful.
Let Israel rejoice in their Maker;
let the people of Zion be glad in their God.
Let them praise God's name in a festive dance;
let them sing praise to God with timbrel and harp.
For God loves the people
and crowns the lowly with victory.
Let the faithful rejoice;
let them sing for joy upon their couches—
let the high praises of God be in their mouths. . . .

. . . This is the glory of all the faithful.
Alleluia.

(Vv. 1–6,9)

Praise

Today we acclaim our gracious God, who has taken on
our flesh in Jesus, as we pray: *Honor and praise be yours*.
- We adore the God who did not shrink from the frailty
  of our humanity, as we pray . . .
- We are filled with awe at the coming of our God in
  the mystery of the Incarnation, as we pray . . .
- Our bruised flesh thrills at the salvation and healing
  of our God found in the birth of Christ, as we pray . . .
- We acclaim the birth of Christ as the brilliant and
  final True Sun of Justice, as we pray . . .
- (Other spontaneous prayers of petition or praise) . . .

Closing

Living God, from your tender mercy the Word has
sprung forth, taking our flesh in the womb of Mary.
Breathe forth your spirit upon us that we may proclaim
the message of this Holy Child all the days of our lives.
We ask this through Christ our salvation. Amen.

EVENING

Thanksgiving

Living God,
we give you thanks and praise this night
for the gift of this most sacred festival.
Your people walked in darkness,
but not without the bright promise of your Christ.
Chained by ancient fears, the nations longed
for the coming of one who would lead them
to liberty and justice.
Dark earth yearned for the coming of a light
that would forever dispel the mists of eternal night.
This night we proclaim
the fulfillment of your promises
in the birth of our Savior.
In every season we praise you
for the mystery of this holy night.
All thanks and praise be yours
through the newborn Christ and the Holy Spirit
forever and ever. Amen.

Psalm 114

Alleluia!
When Israel came forth from Egypt,
from a foreign nation,
Judah became God's temple;
Israel became God's kingdom.
The sea fled at the sight;
the Jordan reversed its course.
The mountains leapt like rams,
and the hills like lambs.
Why was it, sea, that you fled?
Jordan, why reverse your course?
Mountains, why leap like rams;
hills, like lambs?
Tremble, O earth, before Yahweh,
in the presence of God
who turns the rock into a pool
and flint into a spring of water.

Intercessions

As we come to the end of this day of festival, we place before our God the needs of all, as we pray: *Keep us mindful of your love.*

- For all the church, that we may be cleansed of our doubts and fears by this holy season, let us pray . . .
- For those who minister to God's people, that they may be granted the spirit of selfless love, let us pray . . .
- For our gathering in faith, that our love for one another may be the mark of our conversion, let us pray . . .
- For suffering people and all those who are in chains, that they may come to the glory of the newborn Christ, let us pray . . .
- For all who have passed to the promise of God's light and peace, that their companionship may nourish us as we journey, let us pray . . .
- (Other spontaneous prayers of intercession or contrition, or an examination of conscience) . . .

Living God, from your tender mercy the Word has
sprung forth, taking our flesh in the womb of Mary.
Breathe forth your spirit upon us that we may proclaim
the message of this Holy Child all the days of our lives.
We ask this through Christ our hope. Amen.

Closing

1 January:

Mary, Mother of God

Adoration | All praise to you, gracious God,
for the dawning of your Sun of Justice
upon a people that walked in darkness.
In this season, when we set our faces
toward the fullness of your peace,
we rejoice for the life and memory
of Mary, mother of Christ,
whom you consecrated to give birth to the Word.
The Mother of Jesus is the image of your church
and leaven for our discipleship.
She who bore the Promise of the Ages
is the living reminder
that all who profess Jesus as the Christ
must bring the Gospel to birth
until the day of your justice.
All praise and honor be yours
through Christ and the Holy Spirit
forever and ever. Amen.

Psalm 63 | O God, you are my God whom I eagerly seek;
for you my flesh longs and my soul thirsts
like the earth, parched, lifeless, and without water.
I have gazed toward you in the sanctuary
to see your power and your glory.
For your love is better than life;
my lips shall glorify you.
Thus will I praise you while I live;
lifting up my hands, I will call upon your name.
As with the riches of a banquet shall my soul be filled,
and with exultant lips my mouth shall praise you.

On my bed I will remember you,
and through the night watches I will meditate on you:
because you are my help,
and in the shadow of your wings I shout for joy.
My soul clings to you;
your right hand upholds me.

(Vv. 1–8)

With Mary and all the saints, we praise the God of love, **Praise**
as we pray: *Honor and praise, God of love.*
- We worship you, God, who offer peace to all the
  nations, as we pray . . .
- We glorify your name, Holy One, as we pray . . .
- We raise our voices to honor you, immortal God, who
  have given to us a Savior, as we pray . . .
- We are filled with wonder at your mercy, God of
  heaven and earth, as we pray . . .
- (Other spontaneous prayers of petition or praise) . . .

God of all salvation, we give you thanks this day for **Closing**
Mary, model for your people, the church. Fill us with the
grace of the Holy Spirit that like Mary, we may be faithful messengers of Jesus, the word of life. We ask this
through Christ our light and life. Amen.

EVENING

All thanks be to you, God of mercy, **Thanksgiving**
for the gifts that you have bestowed upon us
in Jesus, the light of the world.
As the shades of evening descend upon the earth,
we are grateful for the gift of your brilliant Spirit
who overshadowed Mary, mother of Christ.
In her life, Mary proclaimed a new justice
found only in Christ Jesus.
In your gift of salvation, poor people have their fill;
lowly people are raised to heights never dreamed of.
All praise and thanks be to you
through Christ and the Holy Spirit
forever and ever. Amen.

Psalm 45

My heart overflows with a goodly theme;
I address my verses to the king;
my tongue is like the pen of a ready scribe.
You are the fairest of all;
grace is poured upon your lips;
thus God has blessed you forever.
Gird your sword upon your side, O mighty one,
clothe yourself with glory and majesty!
Hear, O daughter, consider, and turn your ear;
forget your people and your ancestor's home.
The king will desire your beauty.
The people of Tyre are here with gifts,
the richest of the people seeking your favor.
The place of your ancestors your children shall have;
you will make them rulers through all the earth.
I will cause your name to be celebrated in all
generations;
therefore the peoples will praise you forever and ever.
(Vv. 1–3,10–12,16–17)

Intercessions

God has brought us to a new birth and has washed us
clean from all fear in Christ. Let us present our needs to
God, as we pray: *Keep us mindful of your love.*
- For all who acknowledge Jesus as savior, that the
spirit of God may move us to bear the Word to every
nation, let us pray . . .
- For all the nations, that the image of Mary as the
faithful disciple may be leaven of peace and justice,
let us pray . . .
- For our community, that the example of Mary may
strengthen us in our service of one another, let us
pray . . .
- For sick people, suffering people, and all those in
chains, that the devotion of Mary to the suffering
Christ on the cross may be a consolation, let us
pray . . .
- For all those who have died, that Mary, the angels,
Lazarus, and all the saints may welcome them into
Paradise, let us pray . . .
- (Other spontaneous prayers of intercession or contri-
tion, or an examination of conscience) . . .

God of our salvation, we give you thanks this day for Mary, mother of your son and model for your people, the church. Fill us with the grace of the Holy Spirit that like Mary, we may be faithful messengers of Jesus, the word of life. We ask this through Christ our light and life. Amen.

Closing

The Feast
of the Epiphany

MORNING

Adoration
May you be praised, living God,
for the gift of your glorious Light.
As dawn spreads before us,
we lift our voices to acclaim your glory
revealed this day in Christ Jesus.
Today, Christ is made manifest to the nations.
The wise journey from afar to bask in your glory.
To Christ is offered the riches, the fragrance,
and the sorrow of our human flesh.
All praise and honor be yours
through Christ and the Holy Spirit
forever and ever. Amen.

Psalm 72
O God, with your judgment and with your justice,
endow the leaders.
They shall govern your people with justice
and your afflicted ones with righteousness.
The mountains will bring peace for the people,
and the hills justice.
They shall defend the afflicted among the people,
save the children of the poor,
and crush the oppressor.
May they endure as long as the sun
and like the moon through all generations.
They shall be like rain coming down on the field,
like showers watering the earth.
Virtue shall flower in their days,
and world peace till the moon is no more.
Tarshish and the Isles shall offer gifts;
Arabia and Seba shall bring tribute.

All other rulers shall pay homage to them;
all nations shall serve them.

(Vv. 1–7,10–11)

Let us raise our voices to God, as we pray: *Glory to you, gracious and merciful God.*

- We adore you, our God, creator of the universe, as we pray . . .
- We bless you, God, who have sent Christ to be the light of the world, as we pray . . .
- We stand in awe of you, God, who have invited the nations to the cradle of peace, as we pray . . .
- We honor you, God, for granting a new wisdom to the children of earth, as we pray . . .
- (Other spontaneous prayers of petition or praise) . . .

Praise

O God, you have bathed the earth in a new and ever-lasting royalty. Today, we celebrate the coming of Jesus to all humankind. Grant us the gift of wisdom that we may seek the face of your Son all the days of our lives and proclaim the message of the Child to the ends of the earth. We ask this through Christ, the good news. Amen.

Closing

EVENING

Thanksgiving

All-wise God,
we give you thanks and praise
for the wonders of your love and mercy.
Today you have granted to humankind
the fullness of your glory.
Christ Jesus is made manifest,
and the bright lamp that guides us through night
burns radiantly in our midst.
As daylight ends,
we celebrate the victory that is ours in Christ.
The Daystar of your holiness
pierces through the night,
and all people are beckoned toward your light.
The veil of death gives way to immortality,
and the hearts of all the wise are made glad.

All praise and thanks be yours
through Christ and the Holy Spirit
forever and ever. Amen.

Psalm 72
O God, with your judgment and with your justice,
endow the leaders.
They shall govern your people with justice
and your afflicted ones with righteousness.
For they shall rescue the poor when they cry out
and the afflicted when they have no one to help them.
They shall have pity for the needy and the poor;
they shall save the lives of the poor.
From oppression and violence they shall redeem them,
and precious shall their blood be.
To them, long life and continuous prayers;
day by day shall they be blessed.
Blessed be their name forever;
their name shall remain as long as the sun.
In them shall all the nations of the earth be blessed;
all the nations shall proclaim their happiness.
(Vv. 1–2,12–15,17)

Intercessions
The glory of God has been made manifest in Christ. Let
us offer to God the needs of our sisters and brothers, as
we pray: *Keep us mindful of your love.*
- For the church, that we may always make Christ
  manifest in our deeds and words, let us pray . . .
- For all the nations, that they may seek the Christ
  who is the only path to peace and justice, let us
  pray . . .
- For our community, that our love for one another
  may be the sign of the Christ among us, let us pray . . .
- For needy people, that we may wisely offer them the
  gifts of mercy and justice, let us pray . . .
- For the dead, that the Daystar may guide them to
  eternal peace and refreshment, let us pray . . .
- (Other spontaneous prayers of intercession or contrition, or an examination of conscience) . . .

O God, you have bathed all the earth in a new and everlasting royalty. Today, we celebrate the coming of Jesus to all humankind. Grant us the gift of wisdom that we may seek the face of your Son all the days of our lives and proclaim the message of the Child to the ends of the earth. We ask this through Christ, the good news. Amen.

Closing

The Baptism of Jesus

MORNING

Adoration
May you be blessed, adored, and praised,
God of earth and sea and sky
for the kindness you have bestowed upon us
in the gift of Jesus, our salvation.
As daylight dawns,
we celebrate the brilliance of your love,
which dispels the darkness of fear and oppression.
Today Christ plumbed the depths of our humanity,
and you anointed Jesus as the Messiah
in whom you are well-pleased.
All glory and honor be yours
through Christ and the Holy Spirit
forever and ever. Amen.

Psalm 150
Alleluia!
Praise to you, Yahweh, in your sanctuary!
Praise to you in the firmament of your strength.
Praise you for your mighty deeds;
praise you for your sovereign majesty.
Praise to you, Yahweh, with the blast of the trumpet,
praise with lyre and harp.
Praise with timbrel and dance;
praise with strings and flute.
Praise to you, Yahweh, with resounding cymbals;
praise with clanging cymbals.
Let everything that has breath praise Yahweh.
Alleluia.

Praise
As we celebrate the baptism of Jesus, we pray: *Blessed are
you, all-good and loving God.*
• We worship you, God, creator of the world, as we
pray . . .

- We are filled with joy at the coming of God's Son, our salvation, as we pray . . .
- Our spirits rejoice at the salvation, which is ours in Christ, as we pray . . .
- All earth sings of the God who anointed Jesus in the waters of the Jordan, as we pray . . .
- (Other spontaneous prayers of petition or praise) . . .

O God, your love is eternally manifested to us in Christ. As we celebrate the anointing of Christ in the waters of the Jordan, grant us the gift of your Holy Spirit that we may not shrink from the demands of our own baptism. We ask this through Christ our living water. Amen.

Closing

EVENING

Thanksgiving

We give you thanks and praise, God of love,
for the gift of Christ,
who has scattered the shades of darkness and death.
Today we celebrate the baptism of Christ.
We rejoice at the anointing of Jesus
for the service of the world.
In the waters of the Jordan,
human flesh was touched by your divinity,
and the promise of salvation was revealed.
This night and forever,
we give you thanks
for Christ Jesus, our light and peace.
All praise and thanks be yours
through Christ and the Holy Spirit
forever and ever. Amen.

Psalm 110

"Sit at my right hand
until I make your enemies a footstool for your feet."
Yahweh, send forth your mighty scepter from Zion.
Rule in the midst of your enemies!
Your people will offer themselves freely
on the day you lead your host upon the holy mountains.
Like dew from the womb of the dawn
your youth will come to you.
Yahweh has sworn and will not retract:

"You are a priest forever
after the order of Melchizedek."
Yahweh is at your right hand. . . .
Yahweh will drink from the brook by the way,
therefore strengthened and victorious!

(Vv. 1–5,7)

Intercessions

As daylight fades, we celebrate the baptism of Jesus and offer our needs to the God of salvation, as we pray: *Keep us mindful of your love.*

- For the church, that we may be faithful servants of your salvation, which is ours in water and the Spirit, let us pray . . .
- For all those who lead us in faith and government, that the Spirit may make them strong, loving, and wise, let us pray . . .
- For our community, that the waters of salvation might well up in our midst for the service of all, let us pray . . .
- For sick people and all those who thirst for justice, life, and peace, that God may satisfy their every need, let us pray . . .
- For all those who have died, that they may now be washed in the waters of peace and light, let us pray . . .
- (Other spontaneous prayers of intercession or contrition, or an examination of conscience) . . .

Closing

O God, your love is eternally manifested to us in Christ. As we celebrate the anointing of Christ in the waters of the Jordan, grant us the gift of your Holy Spirit that we may not shrink from the demands of our own baptism. We ask this through Christ our living water. Amen.

Ordinary Time

 # Sundays

Thanksgiving

God of all creation,
we give you praise and thanks
for what you have accomplished in our midst.
We come before you grateful
for the death and resurrection of Christ,
your gift of salvation.
From the cross has sprung a fountain of immortality.
From the empty tomb an eternal light
has banished the darkness of death.
Waiting still for Christ to come again,
we offer you our evening sacrifice of praise.
All glory and power be yours,
through Christ and the Holy Spirit,
one God forever and ever. Amen.

Psalm 141

Yahweh, I am calling. Hasten to me;
hear me—I am calling to you.
My prayers rise like incense,
my hands like the evening sacrifice.
Yahweh, set a guard at my mouth,
a watch at the door of my lips.
Do not let my heart be compelled to wrong doing,
to share in the deeds of the evildoers.
No, I will not taste their delights.
A just person may strike me in reproof—
it is kindness;
such a rebuke is oil on my head!
My prayer is ever against the deeds of evildoers.
To you, Yahweh, I turn my eyes.
In you I take shelter—
do not hand me over to death.

Keep me out of traps that are set for me,
from the bait laid for me by evil ones.

(Vv. 1–5,8–9)

At this eventide, let us offer our needs to our God,
creator of the universe, so we pray: *Holy God, hear our
prayer.*
- For the church, that we may be granted the spirit of
  fidelity and love, let us pray . . .
- For all those who serve the Body of Christ, that they
  may be strengthened in their service, let us pray . . .
- For our community, that God may sustain us in truth
  and goodness, let us pray . . .
- For sick and suffering people, that the healing of
  Christ may be their balm, let us pray . . .
- For those who have passed before us in faith, that
  they may come to the peace of heaven, let us pray . . .
- (Other spontaneous prayers of intercession or contri-
  tion, or an examination of conscience) . . .

Merciful God, hear our evening prayer. Send upon us
the gift of your undying light, and keep us faithful to the
end. We ask this through Christ our redeemer. Amen.

Light of all creation,
we give you glory and honor
for raising Jesus into life again.
The dawn of the Resurrection
has broken the bondage of sin
and brought us to the day of your justice.
The memory of the passion of Christ
is the joy of every heart and tongue.
On this day of glad tidings,
we proclaim the majesty of your name,
and offer to you a simple hymn of praise.
All glory be to you
through Christ and the Holy Spirit
forever and ever. Amen.

Intercessions

Closing

MORNING

Adoration

Psalm 63 | O God, you are my God whom I eagerly seek;
for you my flesh longs and my soul thirsts
like the earth, parched, lifeless, and without water.
I have gazed toward you in the sanctuary
to see your power and your glory.
For your love is better than life;
my lips shall glorify you.
Thus will I praise you while I live;
lifting up my hands, I will call upon your name.
As with the riches of a banquet shall my soul be filled,
and with exultant lips my mouth shall praise you.
On my bed I will remember you,
and through the night watches I will meditate on you:
because you are my help,
and in the shadow of your wings I shout for joy.
My soul clings to you;
your right hand upholds me.

(Vv. 1–8)

Praise | Grateful for the gift of the resurrection of Christ, we cry
out: *Glory be to God on high.*

- We celebrate the mercy of God's justice in our midst,
  as we pray . . .
- We honor the glory of God's holy name, as we
  pray . . .
- We praise God who has bound us by the bonds of
  charity, as we pray . . .
- We stand in awe of the wonders of our God, as we
  pray . . .
- (Other spontaneous prayers of petition or praise) . . .

Closing | God of all glory, as we celebrate the resurrection of Jesus
we offer you our morning sacrifice of praise. You are the
justice for the earth. Move us this day to deeds of loving
mercy. We ask this through Christ, the compassionate
one. Amen.

Thanksgiving

All thanks and praise be yours,
God of love eternal,
for having kindled in our midst
the presence of the Risen Christ.
Evening falls upon us.
Yet the darkness of the coming night
bears no fear for us,
for the light of Christ
radiates within our midst
and leads us onward to endless day.
You have drawn us
through this day of the new creation
and now bring us to the hour of our resting.
All glory and honor be yours
through Christ and the Holy Spirit
forever and ever. Amen.

Psalm 110

"Sit at my right hand
until I make your enemies a footstool for your feet."
Yahweh, send forth your mighty scepter from Zion.
Rule in the midst of your enemies!
Your people will offer themselves freely
on the day you lead your host upon the holy mountains.
Like dew from the womb of the dawn
your youth will come to you.
Yahweh has sworn and will not retract:
"You are a priest forever
after the order of Melchizedek."
Yahweh is at your right hand
and will shatter rulers on the day of wrath.
Yahweh will execute judgment among the nations, . . .
scattering them over the earth.
Yahweh will drink from the brook by the way,
therefore strengthened and victorious!

(Vv. 1–6,7)

Intercessions | As evening falls, we bring to our kind God the needs of all the world, as we pray: *Gracious God, have mercy on us.*

- For all Christians, that we may preach the reign of God in word and deed, let us pray . . .
- For the nations, that the peace of God may dispel the rumblings of war, let us pray . . .
- For our community, that our lives may be marked by the spirit of conversion, let us pray . . .
- For all those who suffer, that the resurrection of Christ may be their hope, let us pray . . .
- For the faithful departed, that theirs now may be light, refreshment, and peace, let us pray to the Lord . . .
- (Other spontaneous prayers of intercession or contrition, or an examination of conscience) . . .

Closing | God of all mercy, hear our evening prayer. Forgive us this day for the times when we have been blind to the glory of your countenance. Bring us safely through this night that we may give you praise with the coming of the dawn. We ask this through Christ, the-word-made-flesh. Amen.

Mondays

God of all creation,
the heavens proclaim your glory
and the skies, your wonders.
Jesus is the radiant dawn,
the Word, which is our rule of life,
truth, compassion, and perfect justice.
As daylight breaks,
we give you praise for the gift of Christ
who is forever in our midst,
leading us from sunrise to sunset
to offer you a perfect sacrifice of praise.
All honor and glory be yours,
through Christ and the Holy Spirit
forever and ever. Amen.

Adoration

Harken to my words, O God,
attend to my musing.
Heed my call for help,
to you I pray.
In the morning you hear my voice;
at dawn I will make ready and watch for you.
For you, O God, delight not in wickedness;
no one who is evil remains with you.
The arrogant may not stand in your sight;
you hate all who do futile things.
You destroy all who speak falsehood;
the bloodthirsty and the deceitful you detest.
But I, through your abundant kindness,
will enter your house;
I will worship at your holy Temple
in fear of you.

Psalm 5

(Vv. 1–7)

Praise | We rejoice at the dawn of God's justice, and we pray:
God of truth, we bless your name.
- We gather in praise of God, who scatters the darkness of sin, as we pray . . .
- We come in need of the Spirit who perfects our labors, as we pray . . .
- We confess our need for God's healing, as we pray . . .
- We are drawn by the Spirit to offer our hands for loving service, as we pray . . .
- (Other spontaneous prayers of petition or praise) . . .

Closing | Hear our morning prayer, ever merciful God, and grant that the vision of your reign may be ever in our mind this day. As we return to our daily labor, may your truth be found in our words and deeds. We ask this through Christ our steadfast companion. Amen.

EVENING

Thanksgiving | Loving God of all creation,
it is right that we give you thanks and praise.
Your hands shaped the universe,
and you bless us even in the night,
with a light that never fades.
Darkness gives us no cause for despair,
for the presence of the Risen One
burns brightly in our midst.
In Christ, your glory shines forth
as the bright promise of immortality.
All honor and praise be yours
through Christ and the Holy Spirit
forever and ever. Amen.

Psalm 15 | Yahweh, who has the right to enter your tent,
or to live upon your holy mountain?
Those whose way of life is blameless,
who always do what is right,
who speak the truth from their heart,
whose tongue is not used for slander,
who do no wrong to friends,
cast no discredit on neighbors,
who look with contempt on the reprobate,

but honor those who fear you,
who stand by a pledge at all cost,
who do not ask interest on loans,
and cannot be bribed to exploit the innocent.
If they do all this, nothing can ever shake them.

Gathered in the peace of Christ, let us offer our needs to our God, as we pray: *All-good God, hear our prayer.* | **Intercessions**
- For the unity of all Christians, that we may be re-united in the love of Christ, let us pray . . .
- For all nations, that the liberty of the Gospel may be the foundation of every government, let us pray . . .
- For this gathering of God's people, that our lives may be rooted in the love of Christ, let us pray . . .
- For all those who are held in the chains of suffering, that our saving God will set them free, let us pray . . .
- For all those who have died, that they may now be at peace, let us pray . . .
- (Other spontaneous prayers of intercession or contrition, or an examination of conscience) . . .

All-wise God, your compassion and care have nourished us this day and have led us to night's beginning. Keep the light of your hope burning brightly in your people. We ask this through Christ our liberation. Amen. | **Closing**

Tuesdays

MORNING

Adoration

God of tender mercy,
we praise and thank you for this day of our salvation.
We come before you at this morning hour,
eager to sing of the wonders of your love.
In Christ Jesus,
you have redeemed us from the darkness of death
and brought us into your marvelous light.
Now all creation gives you praise.
Cause of our joy,
we celebrate the wonders of your love
as we accept your will for us this day.
All praise and honor be yours
through Christ and the Holy Spirit
forever and ever. Amen.

Psalm 24

The world and all that is in it belong to Yahweh,
the earth and all who live on it.
Yahweh built it on the deep waters,
laid its foundations in the oceans' depths.
Who has the right to climb Yahweh's mountain?
Or stand in this holy place?
Those who are pure in act and in thought,
who do not worship idols
or make false promises.
Yahweh will bless them.
God their Savior will give them salvation.
Such are the people who come to God,
who come into the presence of our God.
Fling wide the gates,
open the ancient doors,
and the Holy One will come in!
Who is this Holy One?

Yahweh, strong and mighty,
Yahweh, victorious in battle!
Fling wide the gates,
open the ancient doors,
and the Holy One will come in!
Who is this Holy One?
Yahweh, the glorious.

At the dawn of this day, we offer adoration to the God of all that lives, as we pray: *Loving God, we praise your name.*

Praise

- We bless you, God, creator and sustainer, as we pray . . .
- We praise you, Holy Spirit, dwelling in our midst, as we pray . . .
- We give thanks to you, God, for the gift of holy wisdom, as we pray . . .
- We humbly offer thanks for your constant love, even when we turn our backs on you, as we pray . . .
- (Other spontaneous prayers of petition or praise) . . .

Courteous God, hear our morning prayer. May the light of your glory scatter the darkness of sin and death. May your radiance among us herald the coming of your peace to all the world. We ask this through Christ, light of the world. Amen.

Closing

EVENING

We give you thanks,
Source of All Wisdom,
for the blessings and graces
that have been your gift to us this day.
Without the power of your spirit,
confusion and anxiety swirl in our hearts and minds.
In Christ, we live and breathe in the power of your love.
As dusk falls upon us,
we give you thanks and praise
for the radiance of Christ,
which bathes us in the light of eternal hope.

Thanksgiving

All honor and praise be yours
through Christ and the Holy Spirit
forever and ever. Amen.

Psalm 20

May Yahweh answer you in the day of danger;
may the name of the God of Jacob set you up on high.
May God send you help from the sanctuary
and sustain you from Zion.
May God remember all your offerings. . . .
May God grant you what your heart desires
and fulfill all your plans.
May we shout for joy over your triumph
and in the name of our God wave our banners;
may Yahweh fulfill all your petitions.
Now I know that God saves the anointed,
answering from the holy place in heaven
with saving might.
Some boast of chariots and some of horses,
but we boast in the name of our God.
They have bowed down and fallen,
but we have risen and stand firm.
Save us, Yahweh;
answer when we call.

(Vv. 1–3,4–9)

Intercessions

At this eventide, let us offer our needs to God, as we
pray: *God of mercy, hear our prayer.*
- For the church, that we may be moved to pursue
  truth and justice, let us pray . . .
- For all the earth, that we may tend the beauty of
  creation, let us pray . . .
- For our community, those who lead us in faith, and
  for those we serve, let us pray . . .
- For those who suffer from illness, oppression, or
  despair, let us pray . . .
- For those who sleep now in God's embrace, that we
  may one day come with them to the fullness of God's
  reign, let us pray . . .
- (Other spontaneous prayers of intercession or contrition, or an examination of conscience) . . .

Holy God, we give you thanks for having brought us to the end of this day. Let our prayer arise before you and may your blessing descend upon us. We ask this through Christ our salvation. Amen.

Closing

Wednesdays

Adoration

God of the dawn and the dusk,
we adore and worship you
as daylight floods the earth.
You have given us Jesus
as the true teacher of righteousness
and the light of all nations.
We give you praise and thanks
for showering your radiance upon us
and calling us to enter the narrow gate
by deeds of justice and peace.
All glory and adoration be yours
through Christ and the Holy Spirit
forever and ever. Amen.

Psalm 36

Sin speaks to sinners
in the depths of their hearts.
No awe of God is before their eyes.
They so flatter themselves
that they do not know their guilt.
In their mouths are lies and foolishness.
Gone is all wisdom.
They plot the downfall of goodness
as they lie on their beds.
They set their feet on evil ways,
they hold to what is evil.
Your love, Yahweh, reaches to heaven;
your faithfulness to the skies.
Your justice is like a mountain—
your judgments like the deep.
To all creation you give protection.
Your people find refuge
in the shelter of your wings.
They feast on the riches of your house;

they drink from the stream of your delight.
You are the source of life,
and in your light we see light.

(Vv. 1–9)

Praise

We give praise to the God of every season, as we pray:
God of love, may you be blessed.
- We praise you, God, for you have brought us to the
  beginning of this day, as we pray . . .
- We bless God eternal, who refreshes our minds and
  hearts, as we pray . . .
- We adore the countenance of all truth, who is our
  life, as we pray . . .
- We give thanks to you, God, revealed to us in Christ
  Jesus, as we pray . . .
- (Other spontaneous prayers of petition or praise) . . .

Closing

God, your might called Creation from the darkness of
chaos. Hear our prayer this day and protect us from
every evil. Make us witnesses to your glory. We ask this
through Christ our hope. Amen.

EVENING

Thanksgiving

We praise and thank you, God,
for gracing us with every goodness and gift.
Your love is ever present
in the beauty of creation,
in the lives of your daughters and sons,
and in the presence of Christ among us.
We stand at the threshold of the night
grateful for what you have wrought among us
and confident of your protection
in the radiance of Jesus our savior,
who is the light that never fades,
the lamp that is never dimmed in our midst.
All praise and thanks be yours
through Christ and the Holy Spirit
forever and ever. Amen.

Psalm 27

God, you are my light and my salvation;
whom shall I fear?
You are the stronghold of my life;
of whom shall I be afraid?
When evildoers assail me,
uttering slanders against me,
my adversaries and foes,
they shall stumble and fall.
Though a host encamp against me,
my heart will not fear;
though war arise against me,
yet will I be confident.
One thing have I asked of you, Yahweh,
this I seek:
to dwell in your house
all the days of my life,
to behold your beauty
and to contemplate on your Temple.
I believe that I shall see the goodness of Yahweh
in the land of the living!
Wait for Yahweh;
be strong, and let your heart take courage.
Yes, wait for God!

(Vv. 1–4,13–14)

Grateful for the gifts of this day, let us offer our needs to God, as we pray: *May your peace be in our hearts and on our lips.*

- For the church, that our service in Christ may be for the good of all people, let us pray . . .
- For those in government service, that they may be filled with God's peace and justice, let us pray . . .
- For our community, our families, friends, and benefactors, let us pray . . .
- For those whose lives are marred by violence, suffering, or confusion, let us pray . . .
- For all the dead, that they be blessed with the gift of peace, let us pray . . .
- (Other spontaneous prayers of intercession or contrition, or an examination of conscience) . . .

God of heaven and earth, watch over us in love and bring us safely through this night. Keep us vigilant for that day when Christ will come again. We ask this through Christ our holy friend. Amen.

Thursdays

Adoration

Blessed are you, God of all radiance,
for you crowned Jesus with glory and splendor
and gave Christ eternal light for a mantle.
In Christ, you have destroyed the sting of death.
You grace us with your splendor
and make us yearn for the coming of your reign.
The power of your Spirit
is roused in our midst,
and you bid us to tasks of love
for the good of all humankind.
As daylight breaks upon us,
all glory and honor be yours
through Christ and the Holy Spirit
forever and ever. Amen.

Psalm 57

Have mercy on me, God, have mercy.
In you my soul takes shelter;
I take shelter in the shadow of your wings
until the danger passes.
I call out to God the Most High,
to God who has blessed me:
to send from heaven and save me,
to rebuke those who trample me.
May God send me faithfulness and love.
Be exalted above the heavens, God.
Let your glory shine on the earth!
My heart is steadfast, God,
my heart is steadfast;
I mean to sing and play for you.
Awake, my soul
awake, lyre and harp,
I mean to wake the dawn.

Rise high above the heavens, God,
let your glory cover the earth!

(Vv. 1–3,5,7–8,11)

We have been given the light of yet another day. Grate-
fully we cry out: *Loving God, we bless your name.*
- We praise our God who has drawn us together in
  Christ Jesus, as we pray . . .
- We adore the Creator, whose morning star has risen
  in our hearts, as we pray . . .
- We bless the fountain of all mercy, who visits us in
  our distress, as we pray . . .
- We cry out in praise of the Immortal One, whose
  strength is our delight, as we pray . . .
- (Other spontaneous prayers of petition or praise) . . .

Praise

God of all the universe, we give you praise at every
moment of our lives. Dispel from our hearts the darkness
of sin and despair. May your light ever guide our days.
We ask this through Christ, the compassionate one.
Amen.

Closing

EVENING

Thanksgiving

We praise and thank you, creator God.
You gather us here before you
as we come to the end of our labors.
The shades of evening draw closer,
yet you do not give us up to the darkness.
You have kindled in our midst the Christ,
the lamp of hope and the fire of your mercy.
This day has been your gift,
and we offer our hands and hearts to you
for the graces you have bestowed upon us.
Sustain us this night,
and lift us up on eagle's wings
to the safety of your love.
All praise and thanks be yours
through Christ and the Holy Spirit
forever and ever. Amen.

Psalm 30

I praise you, Yahweh, because you have saved me
and kept my enemies from gloating over me.
I cried to you for help, my God,
and you healed me.
You brought me back from the world of the dead.
I was with those who go down to the depths below,
but you restored my life.
Sing praise to Yahweh, you faithful people!
Remember what God has done and give thanks!
Yahweh's anger lasts only a moment,
God's goodness for a lifetime.
There may be tears during the night,
but joy comes in the morning.
I called to you, Yahweh;
I begged for your help.
What good will come from my death?
What profit from my going to the grave?
Are dead people able to praise you?
Can they proclaim your unfailing goodness?
Hear me, Yahweh, and be merciful!
Help me, Yahweh!
You have changed my sadness into a joyful dance;
you have taken off my clothes of mourning
and given me garments of joy.
So I will not be silent;
I will sing praise to you.
Yahweh, you are my God;
I will give thanks to you forever.

(Vv. 1–5,8–12)

Intercessions

From the poverty of our lives, let us call to mind the
needs of all creation and pray: *Gracious God, have mercy.*

- For the church, that we may be ever mindful of God's
  graces to us, let us pray . . .
- For the nations of the world, that the Spirit of holiness may lead all people to peace, let us pray . . .
- For those who seek God in this community, that our
  love for one another may be a witness to the Gospel,
  let us pray . . .
- For all those whose lives are shadowed by poverty and
  distress, that they may come to know the bounty and
  comfort of our God, let us pray . . .

- For the dead, that they may be enfolded into the joys of heaven, let us pray . . .
- (Other spontaneous prayers of intercession or contrition, or an examination of conscience) . . .

God, you illumine the night and order the moon and the stars. Grateful for your presence among us, we ask that you remember us as we pass through the shades of night and journey toward endless day. We ask this through Christ our light. Amen.

Closing

 # Fridays

MORNING

Adoration

Blessed are you,
God, who sends redemption,
for this day of our salvation.
Today we remember the sacrifice of your love
poured out by Jesus on the cross.
In Christ, you did not shrink
from the terror of human dying,
but embraced the ancient fear, which dimmed our eyes
from the light of your hope.
You breathe your spirit this day
into our human hearts
so that all creation may thrill
at the wonders of your love.
All praise and honor be yours
through Christ and the Holy Spirit
forever and ever. Amen.

Psalm 51

In your goodness, O God, have mercy on me;
with gentleness wipe away my faults.
Cleanse me of guilt;
free me from my sins.
My faults are always before me;
my sins haunt my mind.
As you know I was born in guilt,
from conception a sinner at heart.
But you love true sincerity,
so you teach me the depths of wisdom.
Until I am clean, bathe me with hyssop;
wash me until I am whiter than snow.
Create a pure heart in me, O my God;
renew me with a steadfast spirit.
Sacrifices give you no pleasure;
if I offered a holocaust, you would refuse it.

My sacrifice is this broken spirit.
You will not disdain a contrite and humbled heart.
Graciously show your favor to Zion;
rebuild the walls of Jerusalem.

(Vv. 1–3,5–7,10,16–18)

In wonder before the price of our salvation, we acclaim
our God, as we pray: *May we sing your mercies, kind God.*

Praise

- We bless the God whose Son has gained for us true
  freedom, as we pray . . .
- We praise the God whose spirit enlightens our lives,
  as we pray . . .
- We adore the Creator who continually cleanses us
  from sin, as we pray . . .
- We render our gratitude to God for the grace of the
  cross of Christ, as we pray . . .
- (Other spontaneous prayers of petition or praise) . . .

God of the living, the shades of ignorance and fear are
dispelled by the bright dawn, radiating from the wounds
of the crucified Christ. Strengthen us in the Spirit, that,
as Jesus did not shrink from our humanity, we may not
shrink from your invitation to holiness. We ask this
through Christ our salvation. Amen.

Closing

EVENING

We praise and thank you,
Source of Undying Light,
for the victory of Jesus
over the powers of evil and death.
Christ has harrowed hell
and won for all creation
the graces of liberty and justice
and an eternal place
at the seat of your mercy.
This night we proclaim
that the power of death has been broken
and that all flesh has been made new in your sight.
For this gift
we never cease to give you our grateful thanks.

Thanksgiving

All honor and glory be yours
through Christ and the Holy Spirit
forever and ever. Amen.

Psalm 46

God is our refuge and our strength,
our ever-present help in distress.
Though the earth trembles,
and mountains slide into the sea,
we have no fear.
Waters foam and roar,
and mountains shake at their surging;
but the God of hosts is with us—
our stronghold, the God of Israel.
Come! See the deeds of the Most High,
the marvelous things God has done on earth;
all over the world, God has stopped wars—
breaking bows, splintering spears,
burning the shields with fire.
"Be still! and know that I am God,
exalted among the nations, exalted upon the earth."
The Most High is with us;
our stronghold is the God of Israel.

(Vv. 1–3,8–11)

Intercessions

We come before our loving God and offer the needs of
all creation, as we pray: *God of peace, remember us.*
- For the members of the church, that the cross of
  Christ may be our life and witness, let us pray . . .
- For those who lead us in faith and government, that
  the image of the Crucified One may be the inspiration
  of their service, let us pray . . .
- For our community, that the blood of the Lamb may
  cleanse us from sin and make us bold in love, let us
  pray . . .
- For all those whose lives reflect the wounds of the
  Christ crucified, let us pray . . .
- For those who have passed in death from this world,
  that the Lamb of God may guide them to the joys of
  heaven, let us pray . . .
- (Other spontaneous prayers of intercession or contrition, or an examination of conscience) . . .

Faithful God, by the cross of Christ you entered into human suffering and healed the wounds of your people. Receive our evening prayer. Forgive us our sins and prepare us always for the coming of your reign. We ask this through Christ crucified and risen. Amen.

Closing

Saturdays

MORNING

Adoration

God of the universe,
we praise you for scattering the darkness of night
and bringing us to the dawn of your goodness.
Today we honor Mary,
who was inspired to accept
the price of your word.
First she conceived your Word in her heart,
and then in her womb.
She provides a perfect example of discipleship in Christ.
This morning, your radiance breaks forth upon us again,
and, in your light, we see the Light of All the World.
All glory be yours
through Christ and the Holy Spirit
forever and ever. Amen.

Psalm 119

Teach me, O God, the way of your statutes
that I may always observe them.
Give me discernment that I may observe your law
and keep it with all my heart.
Guide me down the path of your commands,
for I delight in it.
Turn my heart to your decrees
and not to love of gain.
Turn my eyes away from seeing worthless things;
by your way renew my life.
Fulfill your promise to your servant—
to those who fear you.
Turn away from me the reproach that I dread,
for your edicts are good.
See, I long for your precepts;
in your justice, give me life.

(Vv. 33–40)

Let us praise God who showers all people in peace, as we pray: *Blessed be the name of God.* | **Praise**
- We praise God, who has called us to a new dignity and freedom, as we pray . . .
- We bless the Author of Life for the gift of this day, as we pray . . .
- We give God thanks for the witness of Mary, the faithful disciple, as we pray . . .
- We praise God for the faith, hope, and love planted in our hearts, as we pray . . .
- (Other spontaneous prayers of petition or praise) . . .

Holy Friend, free us always from the terror of night. May the light of Christ's resurrection ever bathe us in your glory. We ask this through Christ our freedom. Amen. | **Closing**

Lent

Lenten Sundays

Thanksgiving

God of mercy and justice,
we give you thanks and praise
for the gift of Christ Jesus,
who dispels the darkness of sin and oppression.
In this holy season, we journey again
to the fountain of all life
through which we have become your special possession.
Scarred by sin and failure,
we look to your compassion
so that we may know your healing.
All honor and blessing be yours
through Christ and the Holy Spirit
forever and ever. Amen.

Psalm 141

Yahweh, I am calling. Hasten to me;
hear me—I am calling to you.
My prayers rise like incense,
my hands like the evening sacrifice.
Yahweh, set a guard at my mouth,
a watch at the door of my lips.
Do not let my heart be compelled to wrong doing,
to share in the deeds of the evildoers.
No, I will not taste their delights.
A just person may strike me in reproof—
it is a kindness;
such a rebuke is oil on my head!
My prayer is ever against the deeds of evildoers.
To you, Yahweh, I turn my eyes.
In you I take shelter—
do not hand me over to death.

Keep me out of traps that are set for me,
from the bait laid for me by evil ones.

(Vv. 1–5,8–9)

In this season of repentance, we offer our needs to God
as we pray: *God, have mercy on your people.*

- For the church and for all catechumens, that we may
  be open to the grace of conversion, let us pray . . .
- For all nations, that the vision of God's peace may be
  the cornerstone of life itself, let us pray . . .
- For our community, that this Lent may find us hun-
  gering for the reign of God, let us pray . . .
- For all those in need, that the healing of our God
  may be theirs, let us pray . . .
- For those who have died, that they may know the joy
  of heaven, let us pray . . .
- (Other spontaneous prayers of intercession or contrition, or an examination of conscience) . . .

Intercessions

Merciful God, in this Lenten season make our fasting be
acceptable in your sight. May we come to know the
penance that brings liberty to the captives. We ask this
through Christ our redeemer. Amen.

Closing

MORNING

Blessed are you, God of life,
for the light of your compassion,
which has dawned upon us in Jesus.
In this season of penance,
we praise your forgiveness
as we confess the darkness of our sin.
We look to the mystery
of the death and resurrection of Christ
as the hope of all the earth.
All blessing and honor be yours
through Christ and the Holy Spirit
forever and ever. Amen.

Adoration

Psalm 95 | Come, let us sing joyfully to God;
let us acclaim the Rock of our salvation.
Let us greet God with thanksgiving;
let us joyfully sing psalms.
For Yahweh is a great God
above all gods;
God cradles the depths of the earth
and holds fast the mountain peaks.
God shaped the sea and owns it
and formed the dry land by hand.
Come, let us bow down in worship;
let us kneel before the God who made us.
For Yahweh is our God,
and we are the people God shepherds,
the flock God leads.
O that today you would hear God's voice:
"Do not harden your hearts as at Meribah,
as on that day in the desert of Massah
where your ancestors challenged me;
they tested me though they had seen my works.
Forty years with that generation,
and I said: They are a people of
erring heart and they know not my ways.
Therefore I swore in my anger:
They shall not enter into my rest."

Praise | As the Spirit moves within us, we offer praise to our
loving God, as we pray: *Fountain of All Life be praised.*
- We celebrate conversion to the way of God, as we
pray . . .
- We thrill at the end to the reign of sin, as we pray . . .
- We bless the God of all mercy, as we pray . . .
- We rejoice at the coming birth of our sisters and
brothers in baptism, as we pray . . .
- (Other spontaneous prayers of petition or praise) . . .

Closing | Merciful God, in this Lenten season make our fasting be
acceptable in your sight. May we come to know the
penance that brings liberty to the captives. We ask this
through Christ our redeemer. Amen.

Thanksgiving

Almighty and tender God,
we give you thanks and praise as daylight fades.
In this season of our repentance,
we are grateful for the light of Christ,
which guides us through the shades of night.
We offer to you
this sacrifice of love and penance
that we may be steeped again
in the waters of salvation.
All praise and thanks be yours
through Christ and the Holy Spirit
forever and ever. Amen.

Psalm 111

I will thank you, Yahweh, with all my heart
in the meeting of the just and their assembly.
Great are your works
to be pondered by all who love them.
Glorious and sublime are your works;
your justice stands firm forever.
You help us remember your wonders.
You are compassion and love.
You give food to those who fear you,
keeping your covenant ever in mind.
You have shown your might to your people
by giving them the lands of the nations.
Your works are justice and truth;
your precepts are all of them sure;
they are steadfast forever and ever,
made in uprightness and faithfulness.
You have sent deliverance to your people
and established your covenant forever.
Holy your name, greatly to be feared.
To fear you is the beginning of wisdom;
all who do so prove themselves wise.
Your praise shall last forever!

(Vv. 1–10)

Intercessions As darkness descends, we offer our needs to our always patient God, as we pray: *Holy Friend, have mercy.*

- For the church and for all catechumens, that we may be renewed in this season of grace, let us pray . . .
- For those who lead us in faith and government, that they may be people of justice and move us to a life marked by the peace of Christ, let us pray . . .
- For our community, that this season may find us more deeply moved to conversion of life, let us pray . . .
- For all those who suffer, that God's healing touch may be theirs, let us pray . . .
- For the dead, that they may now bask in the light of heaven, let us pray . . .
- (Other spontaneous prayers of intercession or contrition, or an examination of conscience) . . .

Closing Merciful God, in this Lenten season make our fasting be acceptable in your sight. May we come to know the penance that brings liberty to the captives. We ask this through Christ our redeemer. Amen.

Lenten Mondays

All praise to you, God of all providence.
Now is the season of our salvation.
Now is the day of your mercy.
We bow before you in sorrow for sin,
yet confident of your forgiveness.
Be praised for the gift of Christ,
who renews us in mind and heart
and calls us to turn to you with confidence.
All praise and honor is yours
through Christ and the Holy Spirit
forever and ever. Amen.

Adoration

Like the deer that yearns
for running streams,
so my soul is yearning
for you, my God.
My soul is thirsting for God, the living God.
When can I enter to see the face of God?
My tears have become my food night and day,
and I hear it said all day long:
"Where is your God?"
I will remember all these things
as I pour out my soul:
how I would lead the joyous procession
into the house of God,
with cries of gladness and thanksgiving,
the multitude wildly happy.
Why are you so sad, my soul?
Why sigh within me?
Hope in God;
for I will yet praise my savior and my God.

Psalm 42

(Vv. 1–5)

Praise | All praise to our God, who consoles us in this life, as we pray: *God, our guide, we praise your name.*
- We praise our God, who has cleansed us in baptism, as we pray . . .
- We are thankful to God for the generosity of providence, as we pray . . .
- We bless our God for calling us to unity of mind and heart, as we pray . . .
- We stand in awe of the gift of reconciliation with our God, as we pray . . .
- (Other spontaneous prayers of petition or praise) . . .

Closing | Living God, whose salvation is our hope, fill us with the gift of wisdom. Move us to deeds of penance and bring us back to you. We ask this through Christ our salvation. Amen.

EVENING

Thanksgiving | Eternal God,
we give you thanks and praise
for the gift of Christ Jesus,
who enlightens us though daylight fades.
In these days of fasting and repentance,
you stand tenderly near us
that we may come to a new vision of your peace.
You alone are our salvation,
and we cry out to you
through dark times of our life.
All praise and thanks be yours
through Christ and the Holy Spirit
forever and ever. Amen.

Psalm 6 | Yahweh, rebuke me not in your anger,
nor chasten me in your wrath.
Be gracious to me, for I am weak;
heal me, for my heart is troubled.
My soul also is sorely troubled.
Turn and save my life;
deliver me for the sake of your steadfast love,
for in death you are not remembered.
In Sheol who can sing your praise?

I am weary with my moaning;
every night I flood my bed with tears,
I drench my couch with my weeping.
My eyes waste away because of grief;
I grow weak because of my foes.
Leave me, all you worshipers of idols,
for Yahweh has heard the sound of my weeping.
Yahweh has heard my supplication
and accepts my prayer.
All my enemies shall be ashamed and greatly troubled;
they shall turn back and be put to shame in a moment.

Intercessions

God has brought us to salvation in Christ. Let us offer our needs to the living God, as we pray: *Faithful God, hear our prayer.*

- For the church, that we may be cleansed in the memory of our baptism, let us pray . . .
- For those approaching the fountain of salvation, that they may be strengthened for the life of faith, let us pray . . .
- For our community, that this season may find us growing into the fullness of conversion in Christ, let us pray . . .
- For sick and dying people, that God may give them the gift of hope, let us pray . . .
- For all the dead, that God may enfold them in the light of heaven, let us pray . . .
- (Other spontaneous prayers of intercession or contrition, or an examination of conscience) . . .

Closing

God, whose salvation is our hope, fill us with the gift of wisdom. Move us to deeds of penance, and bring us back to you. We ask this through Christ our savior. Amen.

Lenten Tuesdays

MORNING

Adoration | Creator of the universe,
we bless your name as daylight dawns.
The wonder of this day touches
and warms our hearts.
Jesus, your dawn, beckons us to your goodness,
and the chains of sin drop from our limbs.
We desire to build your reign.
All praise and honor be yours
through Christ and the Holy Spirit
forever and ever. Amen.

Psalm 10 | Why do you stand aloof, O God?
Why do you hide yourself in times of trouble?
In arrogance the wicked oppress the poor
who are caught in the schemes
that the wicked have devised.
For the wicked boast of their hearts' desires,
and those greedy for gain curse and renounce you.
The wicked do not seek you, because of their pride;
All their thoughts are, "There is no God."
The ways of the wicked prosper at all times;
your judgments are on high, out of their sight. . . .
Arise, Yahweh! O God, lift up your hand!
Forget not the afflicted!
Yahweh, you will hear the desire of the afflicted;
you will strengthen their hearts; you will incline your ear
to do justice to the orphan and the oppressed,
so that those born of earth may strike terror no more.
(Vv. 1–5,12,17–18)

As this new day calls us to deeds of mercy, we praise the Creator and pray: *God, you are the source of our joy.*

- We praise you, God, for healing us with your love, as we pray . . .
- We give thanks to you, God, for the gift of the Word, as we pray . . .
- We bless you, God, for calling us to life in Christ, as we pray . . .
- We confess our sins and ask for your mercy, gracious God, as we pray . . .
- (Other spontaneous prayers of petition or praise) . . .

Praise

God, we are your grateful children, help us to hear your call in this season of repentance. May your spirit widen our vision to embrace your holy will. We ask this through Christ our savior. Amen.

Closing

EVENING

God of true freedom,
we give you thanks and praise for Christ,
who is the light that scatters our darkness.
When we sinned and turned to evil deeds,
you remained close to us,
calling us back to your grace.
This night and forever,
we are awed by the passion of your love
made manifest in Jesus.
All praise and thanks be yours
through Christ and the Holy Spirit
forever and ever. Amen.

Thanksgiving

Happy those who aid the poor and the lowly.
God will help them when they are in trouble.
Yahweh will protect and preserve them,
will make them happy in the land,
and will not abandon them to the power of their
      enemies.
Yahweh will help them when they are sick
and restore them to health.
I said, "I have sinned against you, God;
be merciful to me and cure me!"

Psalm 41

My enemies speak evil about me.
They say, "When will you die and be forgotten?"
Those who come to see me are not sincere;
they gather all the bad news about me
and then go out and spread it everywhere.
All who hate me whisper together about me;
they imagine the worst about me.
They say, "You are fatally ill
and will never leave your bed again."
Even my best friend—the one I trusted most,
the one who shared my food—
has turned against me.
Be merciful to me, Yahweh,
and restore my health.
I will know that you love me
because they will not triumph over me.
You will help me because I do what is right;
you will keep me in your presence forever.
Let us praise Yahweh,
praise the God of Israel now and forever!
Amen! Amen!

Intercessions

As we come to the end of this Lenten day, let us offer
our needs to God, as we pray: *Incline your ear to us, God,
kind and just.*

- For all Christians, that we may be faithful to the
  discipline of this holy season, let us pray . . .
- For those preparing for entrance into the church, that
  they may be nourished in God's truth, let us pray . . .
- For our community, that this season may find us
  witnessing to the call to conversion in Christ Jesus,
  let us pray . . .
- For all those bereft of hope, that Jesus may guide their
  way to peace, let us pray . . .
- For those who have gone before us in faith, that
  their companionship may inspire and sustain us, let
  us pray . . .
- (Other spontaneous prayers of intercession or contrition, or an examination of conscience) . . .

God, we are your grateful children; help us to hear your call in this season of repentance. May your spirit widen our vision to embrace your holy will. We ask this through Christ our savior. Amen.

Closing

Ash Wednesday and Lenten Wednesdays

MORNING

Adoration

Creator God,
we praise you for choosing us in Christ
to be a holy people, a royal priesthood,
a possession particularly your own.
In Christ you have raised us up on eagle's wings
toward the day of your mercy and compassion.
Reduced to ashes, by the brilliance of your fire,
we offer you our ready hearts
that we may be refreshed by the Fountain of Life.
All praise and honor be yours
through Christ and the Holy Spirit
forever and ever. Amen.

Psalm 12

Help, O Yahweh! for no one now is devout;
faithfulness has vanished from among the people.
People speak falsehood to their neighbor;
with smooth lips and double heart they speak.
May Yahweh destroy all smooth lips,
every boastful tongue—
those who say, "We are strong with our tongues;
our lips are our own. Who rules over us?"
"Because they rob the afflicted, and the needy sigh,
now will I arise," says Yahweh;
"I will grant safety to those who long for it."
The promises of Yahweh are sure,
like tried silver, freed from dross, sevenfold refined.
You will guard us and preserve us always
from this generation,
while about us the wicked strut,
and in high places are the basest of people.

As this Lenten morning dawns, let us honor God, as we pray: *Glory to the God of hope.*

Praise

- We honor you, God, for the promise of a new heaven and a new earth . . .
- We praise you, God, for the gift of the Spirit in our midst, as we pray . . .
- We bless you, God, for the grace of conversion, as we pray . . .
- We adore you, God, for the salvation that has freed us from the power of evil, as we pray . . .
- (Other spontaneous prayers of petition or praise) . . .

Closing

Gracious God, turn your face toward us, and we shall be saved. By the power of the Spirit, may our fasting and penance remind us of the price of the Gospel. We ask this through Christ our hope. Amen.

EVENING

Thanksgiving

Saving God,
we give you praise and thanks as daylight fades.
Christ Jesus has brought us to your right hand.
Your Lamb is the sacrifice for our peace.
From the ashes of our lives,
we raise our hands to you
that we may be renewed in this season of grace.
All praise and thanks be yours
through Christ and the Holy Spirit
forever and ever. Amen.

Psalm 143

God, hear my prayer.
Listen to my plea!
You are just and faithful—
so answer me!
Do not put me, your servant, on trial,
for no one is innocent in your sight.
I remember the days of old.
I ponder all that you have done;
I bring to mind all your deeds.
I stretch out my hands to you in prayer;
like dry ground my soul thirsts for you.
Answer me now, O God.

I have lost all hope!
Do not hide your face from me,
or I will be among those who go down to the land of the
    dead.
You are my God—
teach me to do your will.
May your good spirit
guide me on a safe path.
Save me, O God, as you have promised;
in your justice rescue me from my troubles!
In your faithful love for me, protect me,
because I am your servant.

(Vv. 1–2,5–7,10–12)

Intercessions

In times of trouble and sadness, God will hear our prayer, and so we say: *God, we trust in your gift of grace.*

- For believers everywhere, that the gift of holiness may be ours in the Spirit, let us pray . . .
- For catechumens, that they may hunger for the Word of Life, let us pray . . .
- For our community, that God may bless us with renewal of mind and heart, let us pray . . .
- For people imprisoned by addiction, illness, harmful relationships, or ignorance, that God may set them free, let us pray . . .
- For the dead, that they may rest in God's embrace, let us pray . . .
- (Other spontaneous prayers of intercession or contrition, or an examination of conscience) . . .

Closing

Gracious God, turn your face toward us, and we shall be saved. By the power of the Spirit, may our fasting and penance remind us of the price of the Gospel. We ask this through Christ our hope. Amen.

Lenten Thursdays

Blessed are you,
God of heaven and earth,
for the gift of the dawn,
which brings us to the day's beginning.
In Christ, you have made us
your people and your inheritance,
setting us apart as a holy nation.
We offer to you our morning praise
and dedicate our works of penance
in honor of your justice and mercy.
All praise and honor be yours
through Christ and the Holy Spirit
forever and ever. Amen.

Psalm 32

Happy are those whose fault is taken away,
whose sin is covered.
Happy those whose sin Yahweh does not count,
in whose spirit there is no guile.
As long as I would not speak,
my bones wasted away with groaning all day long;
for day and night your hand lay heavy upon me.
My strength was dried up as by the summer's heat.
Then I acknowledged my sin to you,
and did not cover my guilt.
I said, "I confess my faults to you,"
and you took away the guilt of my sin.
For this shall all the faithful pray to you in time of stress.
Though deep waters rise,
they shall not reach them.
You are my shelter;
you will protect me from trouble
and surround me with songs of deliverance.

I will instruct you
and show you the way you should walk;
I will counsel you and watch over you.
Do not be senseless like horses or mules,
their tempers curbed only by bridle and bit,
or they will not come near you.
Many are the sorrows of the wicked,
but faithful love surrounds those who trust in you.
Rejoice and be glad in Yahweh, you just;
exult, all you upright of heart.

Praise

As the Body of Christ, we proclaim the God of all mercy, as we pray: *Saving God, we praise you this day.*
- We are thankful for the mercy of God that has gathered us together, as we pray . . .
- We wonder at the healing brought to our heart when we believe in Christ Jesus, as we pray . . .
- We stand in awe of the freely given love of God, which is ours, as we pray . . .
- We are grateful for the gift of this day of penance, as we pray . . .
- (Other spontaneous prayers of petition or praise) . . .

Closing

God of tender mercies, without the presence of your spirit we live in fear and emptiness. Bless our works of penance, and gather us into the fullness of Easter joy. We ask this through Christ our joy. Amen.

EVENING

Thanksgiving

Thanks to you, living God,
for the presence of Christ in our midst.
You shelter your church
beneath the comfort of your wings.
Sinners though we are,
we can hope in the bright promise of immortality,
which is ours in Christ Jesus.
All praise and thanks be yours
through Christ and the Holy Spirit
forever and ever. Amen.

By the rivers of Babylon
we sat and wept, remembering Zion.
On the poplars of that land
we hung up our harps;
there our captors asked of us
the lyrics of our songs
and urged us to be joyous:
"Sing for us one of the songs of Zion!" they said.
How could we sing a song of Yahweh
while in a foreign land?
If I forget you, Jerusalem,
may my right hand forget its skill!
May my tongue cleave to the roof of my mouth
if I forget you,
if I do not consider Jerusalem
my greatest joy.
Remember, Yahweh, what the Edomites did
that day in Jerusalem.
When they said, "Tear it down,
tear it down to its foundations!"
O daughter of Babylon—you destroyer—
happy those who shall repay you
the evil you have done us!

(Vv. 1–8)

Psalm 137

Gathered as one body, we entrust our needs to God, as
we pray: *Hear our prayer, ever-present God.*
- For the church and for all catechumens, that the love
  of Christ may be the center of our lives, let us pray . . .
- For all people, that through Christ we may be agents
  of reconciliation in a divided world, let us pray . . .
- For our community, that this season may find us
  renewed in spirit and in truth, let us pray . . .
- For those held in the bondage of sin, that Jesus the
  liberator may break their chains, let us pray . . .
- For those who have passed before us, that they may
  know the peace of Christ, which is beyond all understanding, let us pray . . .
- (Other spontaneous prayers of intercession or contrition, or an examination of conscience) . . .

Intercessions

Closing   God of tender mercies, without the presence of your spirit we live in fear and emptiness. Bless our works of penance and gather us into the fullness of Easter joy. We ask this through Christ our joy. Amen.

Lenten Fridays

Adoration

Blessings to you, our God,
before whom angels and ancients fall prostrate.
As daylight dawns,
we gather in the living memory
of Jesus, the suffering servant
by whose wounds we have been healed.
Jesus, embracing our humanity,
has made the tree of suffering
the sign of your eternal victory.
For the wonder of this gift sealed in Jesus' blood,
we give you praise and glory
through Christ and the Holy Spirit
forever and ever. Amen.

Psalm 51

In your goodness, O God, have mercy on me;
with gentleness wipe away my faults.
Cleanse me of guilt;
free me from my sins.
My faults are always before me;
my sins haunt my mind.
As you know I was born in guilt,
from conception a sinner at heart.
But you love true sincerity,
so you teach me the depths of wisdom.
Until I am clean, bathe me with hyssop;
wash me until I am whiter than snow.
Create a pure heart in me, O God;
renew me with a steadfast spirit.
Sacrifices give you no pleasure;
if I offered a holocaust, you would refuse it.
My sacrifice is this broken spirit.
You will not disdain a contrite and humbled heart.

Graciously show your favor to Zion;
rebuild the walls of Jerusalem.

(Vv. 1–3,5–7,10,16–18)

Praise

Awed by the sign of the cross and the blood of the Lamb,
we cry out this day: *Bless God, who heals all hearts.*

- We are filled with gratitude for the free gift of salvation, as we pray . . .
- We are thankful for the presence of the Spirit who strengthens us in our fasting, as we pray . . .
- We bless God, whose mercy is our hope, as we pray . . .
- We praise our God, whose light has put darkness to flight, as we pray . . .
- (Other spontaneous prayers of petition or praise) . . .

Closing

Holy and Immortal One, we stand bathed in the blood of Christ, which washes away our sin and guilt. We are grateful for the gift of salvation, which is ours through the obedience of Jesus to your holy will. May we be renewed in this season of repentance and deepened in our Easter faith. We ask this through Christ our brother. Amen.

EVENING

Thanksgiving

God present with us,
your love terrifies the powers of darkness.
We give you praise and thanks
for the presence of the Crucified One,
who is the light of all creation.
In obedience to your will,
Jesus died so that eternal life might be revealed.
From the terrifying fear
that was the shadow of the cross,
a new hope has been born.
All glory and thanksgiving be yours
through Christ and the Holy Spirit
forever and ever. Amen.

Psalm 130

Out of the depths I cry to you, O God.
God, hear my voice!

Let your ears be attentive
to my cry for mercy.
If you, O God, mark our guilt,
who can stand?
But with you is forgiveness;
and for this we revere you.
I trust in you, O God,
my soul trusts in your word.
My soul waits for you, O God.
More than sentinels wait for the dawn,
let Israel wait for you.
For with you is faithful love
and plentiful redemption.
You will redeem Israel
from all their iniquities.

Intercessions

Grateful for the salvation that has been won for us at
the cross, we bring our needs to you, God, as we pray:
Holy God, receive our prayer.
- For the church, that we may serve always in the
  memory of the cross, let us pray . . .
- For those who journey toward the Fountain of Life in
  this Lenten season, that their faith may grow strong
  and deep, let us pray . . .
- For our community, that the blood of the Lamb may
  cleanse us from every sin, let us pray . . .
- For those ensnared by addiction, abusive relationships, poverty, or ignorance, that the Spirit may move
  us to their service, let us pray . . .
- For those who have died, that their present journey
  may be guided by the bright wisdom of God, let us
  pray . . .
- (Other spontaneous prayers of intercession or contrition, or an examination of conscience) . . .

Closing

Holy and Immortal One, we stand bathed in the blood
of Christ, which washes away our sin and guilt. We are
grateful for the gift of salvation, which is ours through
the obedience of Jesus to your holy will. May we be
renewed in this season of repentance and deepened in
our Easter faith. We ask this through Christ our brother.
Amen.

Lenten Saturdays

Adoration

You, God, are the balm of every sorrow.
As daylight breaks upon us,
we give you praise and bless your name.
Filled with sorrow at the sin of the world,
we stand with the Mother of Christ
at the foot of the cross.
With her and with all believers,
we proclaim and confess
your goodness and mercy,
which have brought an end
to darkness and despair.
All praise and glory be yours
through Christ and the Holy Spirit
forever and ever. Amen.

Psalm 88

Yahweh, my God, I call for help all day;
I cry out to you all night.
May my prayer come to you.
Hear my cries for help
for my soul is troubled;
my life draws near to Sheol.
I am counted among those
who, without strength, go down to the pit.
I am alone, down among the dead,
among the slain in their graves—
among those you have forgotten,
those deprived of your care.
But I am here, pleading for your help,
waiting for you every morning.
O God, why do you reject me?
Why do you hide your face from me?
I am afflicted and have suffered since my youth;
I bore your fury; now I almost despair.

You have turned my friends and neighbors against me;
now darkness is my only friend.

(Vv. 1–5,13–15,18)

Praise

With Holy Mary and all creation, we praise the God of
salvation, as we pray: *God of hope, we give you praise.*
- We are thankful to God for our salvation in Christ, as
  we pray . . .
- We offer our gratitude for the graces of this season, as
  we pray . . .
- We wonder at God's love, which has called us to new
  life, as we pray . . .
- We are awed by the mercy of God, which is our
  healing, as we pray . . .
- (Other spontaneous prayers of petition or praise) . . .

Closing

Loving God, whose consolation refreshes our parched
spirits, bring us back to you and deepen our faith in your
crucified and victorious Servant. We ask this through
Christ our salvation. Amen.

Passion Sunday (Palm Sunday)

Thanksgiving

Merciful God,
this night we give you praise and thanks
for the gift of Christ, who is our ransom from sin.
Not by silver and gold,
but by the blood of the Lamb have we been saved.
This night we enter into these most sacred days,
during which we remember
the death and resurrection of Jesus the Christ.
Through the shades of night, our hearts are joyful
for the presence of the Crucified One,
who leads us onward
to the new and final day of your justice.
All glory and thanksgiving be yours
through Christ and the Holy Spirit
forever and ever. Amen.

Psalm 141

Yahweh, I am calling. Hasten to me;
hear me—I am calling to you.
My prayers rise like incense,
my hands like the evening sacrifice.
Yahweh, set a guard at my mouth,
a watch at the door of my lips.
Do not let my heart be compelled to wrong doing,
to share in the deeds of the evildoers.
No, I will not taste their delights.
A just person may strike me in reproof—
it is a kindness;
such a rebuke is oil on my head!
My prayer is ever against the deeds of evildoers.
To you, Yahweh, I turn my eyes.

In you I take shelter—
do not hand me over to death.
Keep me out of traps that are set for me,
from the bait laid for me by evil ones.

(Vv. 1–5,8–9)

As we enter into the mystery of the passion of Christ, | **Intercessions**
we offer our needs to God, as we pray: *God immortal,*
hear our prayer.

- For all Christians, that this holiest of weeks may be a season of true renewal, let us pray . . .
- For all catechumens, that their journey to the Fountain of Life may be a witness of peace to the whole church, let us pray . . .
- For our community, that these days may find us more deeply renewed in the mystery of the cross, let us pray . . .
- For those who are held in the bondage of despair, that the passion of the Messiah may be their freedom, let us pray . . .
- For those who have passed from this world, that the victory of Christ may be their light and guide to heaven, let us pray . . .
- (Other spontaneous prayers of intercession or contrition, or an examination of conscience) . . .

Eternal God, the obedience of Jesus led him to embrace | **Closing**
the terror of death on the cross. May the passion of
Christ teach us to embrace your holy will for us. We ask
this through Christ our redemption. Amen.

MORNING

Adoration

Blessed are you, God of our salvation,
for the victory of Christ, our peace.
Today, Jesus enters Zion.
The children of Israel are filled with joy,
and the very stones burst forth in praise
at the coming of the Blessed One.
Jesus, riding on a beast of labor,

carries the burden of our sins
and brings us to the brilliance and eternal dawn
of the new Jerusalem, the city of everlasting peace.
All praise and glory be yours
through Christ and the Holy Spirit
forever and ever. Amen.

Psalm 24

The world and all that is in it belong to Yahweh,
the earth and all who live on it.
Yahweh built it on the deep waters,
laid its foundations in the oceans' depths.
Who has the right to climb Yahweh's mountain?
Or stand in this holy place?
Those who are pure in act and in thought,
who do not worship idols
or make false promises.
Yahweh will bless them.
God their Savior will give them salvation.
Such are the people who come to God,
who come into the presence of our God.
Fling wide the gates,
open the ancient doors,
and the Holy One will come in!
Who is this Holy One?
Yahweh, strong and mighty,
Yahweh, victorious in battle!
Fling wide the gates,
open the ancient doors,
and the Holy One will come in!
Who is this Holy One?
Yahweh, the glorious.

Praise

Christ has entered Jerusalem and the mystery of our
salvation is at hand. We cry out in joy: *Saving God, we
give you praise.*

- We worship the One who has saved us in Christ, as
  we pray . . .
- We honor the God who calls all peoples to freedom,
  as we pray . . .
- We bless our God, who leads us to the heavenly
  Jerusalem, as we pray . . .

- We thank our God, who offers mercy to sinners, as we pray . . .
- (Other spontaneous prayers of petition or praise) . . .

Eternal God, the obedience of Jesus led him to embrace the terror of death on the cross. May the passion of Christ teach us to embrace your holy will for us. We ask this through Christ our redemption. Amen.

Closing

SECOND EVENING

Thanksgiving

All glory and thanksgiving be yours,
God of light,
for the radiance of Christ Jesus
through whom the darkness of night
has lost all power.
Jesus did not shrink from the terror of death.
Obedient to your will,
Christ has brought us to victory
at your right hand,
and we have been healed of every wound.
In the blood of Christ, sinful earth rejoices
and the gift of your justice has been sealed.
All honor and thanksgiving be yours
through Christ and the Holy Spirit
forever and ever. Amen.

"Sit at my right hand
until I make your enemies a footstool for your feet."
Yahweh, send forth your mighty scepter from Zion.
Rule in the midst of your enemies!
Your people will offer themselves freely
on the day you lead your host upon the holy mountains.
Like dew from the womb of the dawn
your youth will come to you.
Yahweh has sworn and will not retract:
"You are a priest forever
after the order of Melchizedek."
Yahweh is at your right hand
and will shatter rulers on the day of wrath.

Psalm 110

Yahweh will execute judgment among the nations, . . .
scattering them over the earth.
Yahweh will drink from the brook by the way,
therefore strengthened and victorious!

Intercessions We have entered into these sacred days when we remember the mysteries of faith. Let us offer our needs to God, as we pray: *Hear our prayer, living God.*

- For the church, that these sacred days may be the season of our renewal, let us pray . . .
- For all who are approaching the waters of baptism, that they may persevere to the end, let us pray . . .
- For our community, that the blood of the Lamb may inspire us to a life of service, let us pray . . .
- For people captive to addiction, abusive relationships, illness, or ignorance, that the Just One may set them free, let us pray . . .
- For all those who have died, that we may faithfully remember them until all peoples are brought to the gates of the new and eternal Jerusalem, let us pray . . .
- (Other spontaneous prayers of intercession or contrition, or an examination of conscience) . . .

Closing Eternal God, the obedience of Jesus led him to embrace the terror of death on the cross. May the passion of Christ teach us to embrace your holy will for us. We ask this through Christ our redemption. Amen.

The Sacred Triduum

Holy Thursday

Thanksgiving

All praise and thanks be yours, God of mercy.
You have sent Christ Jesus,
whose obedience to your will
has brought us from darkness to eternal light.
On this holy night, we enter into the mystery
of the death and resurrection of Jesus.
Your Suffering Servant washed the feet of the Apostles,
giving us an example of how we are to serve,
and made of us a holy people, a royal priesthood.
Your church, built upon both charity and justice,
heralds the victory of Jesus to the ends of the earth.
As Jesus entered the Garden
and offered you the sacrifice of obedience,
so we raise our hands in thanksgiving
for this mystery of living light.
All glory and thanks be yours
through the Crucified One and the Holy Spirit
forever and ever. Amen.

Psalm 145

I sing your praises, O my God,
and I will praise your name forever and ever.
Every day will I bless you,
and I will praise your name forever and ever.
Great are you, Yahweh, and most worthy of praise;
your greatness is beyond our understanding.
Generation after generation
praises your work and proclaims your might.
They speak of your splendor and glorious renown
and proclaim your wondrous works.
They discourse on the power of your wonderful deeds
and declare your greatness.
They publish the fame of your abundant goodness
and joyfully sing of your justice.

Yahweh, you are gracious and compassionate,
slow to anger and full of love.
You lift up all who are falling
and raise up all who are bowed down.
The eyes of all look hopefully to you,
and you give them bread in due season.
You open your hand
and satisfy the desire of every living thing.
May my mouth speak your praise, Yahweh,
and may all creatures bless your holy name forever and
    ever.

(Vv. 1–8,14–16,21)

Intercessions

This night is the beginning of our salvation. Let us
offer our needs to our compassionate God, as we pray:
Gracious God, have mercy.
- For the church, that we may be the living communion
  of the love of God, let us pray . . .
- For catechumens and penitents, that they may be
  strengthened in their journey of faith, let us pray . . .
- For our community, that we may follow the example
  of the One who came to serve, let us pray . . .
- For sick and suffering people, that the agony of
  Christ in the Garden may be their consolation, let us
  pray . . .
- For those who have passed from the turmoil of this
  life, that the victory of heaven may be theirs, let us
  pray . . .
- (Other spontaneous prayers of intercession or contrition, or an examination of conscience) . . .

Closing

O God, we enter this night into the mystery of faith. As
Christ Jesus has cleansed us by his selfless love, may your
spirit enliven us to celebrate the cross and the Resurrection. We ask this through Christ our redeemer. Amen.

Good Friday

Adoration

Compassionate God,
as daylight dawns,
we fall prostrate before your majesty and glory.
From the beginning of creation,
you did not abandon us to the ancient curse,
but gave the promise of a redeemer to us,
a savior who would manifest your complete love for us.
This day we look to Calvary
and stand in awe
of the sacrifice of your obedient and suffering Servant.
Raised up for us upon the horror of that tree,
Jesus has healed us by his wounds.
This is the day of our salvation,
and for it we give you praise
through the crucified Christ and the Holy Spirit
forever and ever. Amen.

Psalm 22

My God, my God, why have you deserted me?
Far from my prayer, from the words I cry?
I call all day, my God, but you never answer;
all night long I call and cannot rest.
Yet, Holy One,
you who make your home in the praises of Israel—
in you our ancestors put their trust;
they trusted and you rescued them.
They called to you for help and were saved;
they never trusted you in vain.
Yet here I am, now more worm than human,
scorn of all, jest of the people.
All who see me jeer at me;
they toss their heads and sneer:
"You relied on Yahweh, let Yahweh save you!
If Yahweh is your friend, let Yahweh rescue you!"

Yet you drew me out of the womb;
you entrusted me to my mother's breasts.
You placed me on your lap from my birth,
from my mother's womb you have been my God.
Do not stand aside: trouble is near
and I have no one to help me!

(Vv. 1–11)

Praise

In awe before the mystery of the Cross, we cry out:
Have mercy on us, compassionate God.
- Christ has come to endure suffering for our sake, so
  we pray . . .
- Christ has conquered death, so we pray . . .
- Christ has drawn all creation to the throne of mercy,
  so we pray . . .
- Christ was obedient unto death, even to death on a
  cross, so we pray . . .
- (Other spontaneous prayers of petition or praise) . . .

Closing

God of mercy, we stand in the shadow of the cross and
contemplate in holy fear the price of our salvation. Keep
us faithful to the Crucified One, that we may proclaim
your justice to all the nations. We ask this through
Christ our liberator. Amen.

EVENING

Thanksgiving

All praise and thanks to you, God of the universe,
for the gift of salvation that is ours this day.
Jesus the Christ, the silent and innocent lamb,
has been struck down for us in love.
Upon the terrible figure of the cross,
sinful humanity has been drawn to you.
Jesus, held within the arms of his sorrowful mother,
has embraced the sting of death,
and we have been given the gift of eternal hope.
This is the wondrous gift of your love,
the mark of our faith,
and the hope of those approaching the Fountain of Life.
All glory and thanks to you
through the crucified Christ and the Holy Spirit
forever and ever. Amen.

Psalm 22

A pack of dogs surrounds me;
a gang of villains closes in on me.
They tie me hand and foot
and leave me lying in the dust of death.
I can count every one of my bones;
they glare and gloat over me.
They divide my garments among them
and cast lots for my clothes.
Do not stand aside, Yahweh.
O my strength, come quickly to my help;
rescue my soul from the sword,
my life from the grip of the dog.
Save me from the lion's mouth,
my poor soul from the wild bulls' horns!
Then I shall proclaim your name,
praise you in full assembly:
"You who fear Yahweh, praise God!
Entire race of Abraham and Sarah, glorify God!
Entire race of Israel, revere God!
For Yahweh has not despised
or disdained the poor in their poverty,
has not hidden from them,
but has answered when they called."

(Vv. 16–24)

Intercessions

In the quiet of the dusk, we stand in awe at the sacrifice of the Innocent Lamb. In this spirit, we offer our needs to God, as we pray: *God immortal, grant us peace.*

- For the church, that we may be ever grateful for the price of our redemption, let us pray . . .
- For catechumens, that the death of Jesus may inspire them to a life of service in Christ's name, let us pray . . .
- For our community, that the cross of Jesus may be the sign of our love of one another, let us pray . . .
- For all those who suffer, that the Passion of Christ may be their consolation and hope, let us pray . . .
- For the dead, that the Passover of Christ may carry them to the peace of heaven, let us pray . . .
- (Other spontaneous prayers of intercession or contrition, or an examination of conscience) . . .

God of mercy, we stand in the shadow of the cross and
contemplate in holy fear the price of our salvation. Keep
us faithful to the Crucified One, that we may proclaim
your justice to all the nations. We ask this through
Christ our liberator. Amen.

Closing

Holy Saturday

Adoration

All glory be yours, God of all compassion.
As daylight dawns,
we gather in the shadow of the tomb of Christ,
mindful of the price of our redemption.
In the silence of our memorial,
we call to mind the immensity of your love,
and we are filled with awe and wonder.
In the face of Christ's death,
we do not despair, but are filled with hope
that your promise of eternal life will be fulfilled.
Christ has vanquished hell,
and we acknowledge that you are the God of the living.
All praise and glory be yours
through the crucified Christ and the Holy Spirit
forever and ever. Amen.

Psalm 103

Bless Yahweh, O my soul.
Bless God's holy name, all that is in me!
Bless Yahweh, O my soul,
and remember God's faithfulness:
in forgiving all your offenses,
in healing all your diseases,
in redeeming your life from destruction,
in crowning you with love and compassion,
in filling your years with good things,
in renewing your youth like an eagle's.
Yahweh does justice
and always takes the side of the oppressed.
God's ways were revealed to Moses,
and Yahweh's deeds to Israel.

Yahweh is merciful and forgiving,
slow to anger, rich in love;
Yahweh's wrath does not last forever;
it exists a short time only.
Bless Yahweh, all nations,
servants who do God's will.
Bless Yahweh, all creatures
in every part of the world.
Bless Yahweh, O my soul.

(Vv. 1–9,21–22)

Praise

In awe before the mystery of the cross and the silence of
the tomb, we cry out: *Have mercy, God who gives new life.*
- Christ has come to endure suffering for our sake, so
  we pray . . .
- Christ has conquered death, so we pray . . .
- Christ has drawn all things to the throne of mercy, so
  we pray . . .
- Christ was obedient unto death, even to death on a
  cross, so we pray . . .
- (Other spontaneous prayers of petition or praise) . . .

Closing

God of mercy, we stand in the mystery of the cross and
tomb, and we contemplate in holy fear the price of our
salvation. Keep us faithful to the Crucified One, that we
may proclaim your justice to all the nations. We ask this
through Christ our redemption. Amen.

EVENING

Thanksgiving

All praise and thanks to you, eternal God,
for the gift of your Crucified One,
who has released the just from the chains of hell.
As daylight fades, we rejoice
in the sacrifice of your obedient and suffering Servant.
By the cross of Christ,
you have destroyed death
and the power of the Evil One.
This night, with those to be reborn in baptism,
we prepare for the celebration of our Passover,
and we are eager for the Resurrection
to set fire to our minds and hearts.

Longing for the flame of justice,
we give you thanks and praise
through the crucified Christ and the Holy Spirit
forever and ever. Amen.

Psalm 102

My days pass away like shadows;
I wither away like grass.
But you, Yahweh, endure forever;
every age remembers you!
Rise! Forgive Zion!
Pity Zion, for it is time—
at last the hour has come.
Your servants love even Zion's stones
and are moved to pity by the city's dust.
Then the nations will revere your name, Yahweh,
and all the rulers on earth will respect your glory
when you found Zion anew
and then appear in glory.
Yahweh, you will answer the prayer of the helpless
and will not laugh at their plea.
Record this for future generations
so that people not born yet can praise God.
Yahweh has leaned down from the sanctuary's heights,
and has gazed down at earth from the heavens
to hear the groans of the prisoners
and to liberate those doomed to die.

(Vv. 11–20)

Intercessions

As we eagerly await this Easter vigil, we raise our needs
to God, as we pray: *Have mercy on us, God of endless
glory.*

- For the church, that our faithful watching at the
  tomb of Christ may bring us to the fullness of Easter
  joy, let us pray . . .
- For catechumens throughout the world, that the
  silent wonder of this night may bring them to the
  exultant joy of salvation, let us pray . . .
- For our community, that our watching may deepen
  the renewal of our life in the Risen Christ, let us
  pray . . .

- For those whose lives are bereft of hope and peace, that the coming feast of the Resurrection may be their hope, let us pray . . .
- For the dead, that Christ may lead them to the fullness of light, peace, and happiness, let us pray . . .
- (Other spontaneous prayers of intercession or contrition, or an examination of conscience) . . .

Closing

God of mercy, we stand in the mystery of the cross and tomb and we contemplate in holy fear the price of our salvation. Keep us faithful to the Crucified One that we may proclaim your justice to all the nations. We ask this through Christ our redemption. Amen.

Easter

The Sundays of Easter and the Octave

FIRST AND
SECOND
EVENING

Thanksgiving

All praise and thanks be yours, compassionate God,
for the bright fire of your love,
which is kindled in our midst.
Jesus, the lamp of your goodness,
leads us from the beginning of night
to the dawning of your final day.
As the shades of dusk descend upon us,
our hearts rejoice,
for the ramparts of fear and evil
have crumbled before the victory of our Messiah.
All praise and thanks be yours
through the Risen Christ and the Holy Spirit
forever and ever. Amen.

Psalm 116

I love you, Yahweh, because you have heard
my voice and my supplications,
because you have inclined your ear to me.
Therefore I will call on you as long as I live.
The cords of death encompassed me;
the pangs of Sheol laid hold on me;
I suffered sorrow and anguish.
Then I called on your name, Yahweh:
"Oh Yahweh, I beseech you, save my life!"
Gracious are you, Yahweh, and righteous;
you are full of compassion.
You protect the simplehearted;
when I was brought low, you saved me.
Be at rest once more, O my soul,
for Yahweh has been good to you.

140

For you, Yahweh, have delivered my soul from death,
my eyes from tears,
my feet from stumbling.
I walk before you, Yahweh,
in the land of the living.

(Vv. 1–9)

We gather this night, as did the early disciples, searching
for the peace of Christ, which surpasses all understanding. In this spirit, we offer our needs, as we pray: *Grant
us, God, eternal peace.*

Intercessions

- For the church and the newly baptized, that the
  Easter season may find us refreshed by the waters of
  baptism, let us pray . . .
- For those who serve us in faith and government, that
  they may be inspired and nourished by the selfless
  power of the Resurrection, let us pray . . .
- For our community, that we may share the light of
  Christ with all we meet, let us pray . . .
- For all those who live in fear, confusion, anxiety, and
  addiction, that the power of the Risen One may
  break their chains, let us pray . . .

- For all the dead, that the brilliance of the victorious Christ may lead them to the glory of life eternal, let us pray . . .
- (Other spontaneous prayers of intercession or contrition, or an examination of conscience) . . .

Closing | God of all creation, in obedience to your holy will, Jesus embraced our humanity. You raised him from the dead to the glory of eternal life. In this season, bathe us in the light of Christ and lead us to the eternal vision of your beauty. We ask this through Christ our savior. Amen.

MORNING

Adoration | Blessed are you, creator God,
for the salvation of Christ,
which has dawned upon us
and set us free
from the darkness of sin and death.
Today, the sorrow of the cross
has been consumed
by the bright promise of the empty tomb.
Christ is risen from the dead,
and all creation thrills and basks
in the light of your victorious love.
All praise and glory be yours
through the Risen Christ and the Holy Spirit
forever and ever. Amen.

Psalm 118 | Alleluia!
I give thanks to you, Yahweh, for you are good;
your love is everlasting!
Let the house of Israel say,
"Your love is everlasting!"
Let the House of Aaron say,
"Your love is everlasting!"
Let those who fear Yahweh say,
"Your love is everlasting!"
In desperation I called to you, Yahweh;
you heard me and came to my aid.
With Yahweh at my side helping me,
what can anyone do to me?

With Yahweh on my side, best help of all,
I can triumph over my enemies.
I would rather take refuge in you, Yahweh,
than rely on people;
I would rather take refuge in you, Yahweh,
than rely on rulers.

(Vv. 1–9)

As the dawn of the Resurrection bathes us in hope, let us praise our God as we say: *God of life, all praise be yours.* | **Praise**
- We give thanks to God for the gift of the Resurrection, as we pray . . .
- We wonder at the depths of the love of God in our midst, as we pray . . .
- We give thanks to God for our salvation in the blood of the Lamb, as we pray . . .
- We stand in awe before the justice of God, which sets us free, as we pray . . .
- (Other spontaneous prayers of petition or praise) . . .

God of all creation, in obedience to your holy will, Jesus embraced our humanity. You raised him from the dead to the glory of eternal life. In this season, bathe us in the light of Christ and lead us to the eternal vision of your beauty. We ask this through Christ our savior. Amen. | **Closing**

Easter Mondays Outside the Octave

Adoration

Praise and blessings to you,
God of all glory,
for the gift of light,
which is our salvation in the Risen Christ.
As daylight breaks,
we gather in the living memory of your justice
poured out for us in Christ
and raised up to your seat of mercy.
The wounds of the Crucified One
have become the fountain of peace.
The blind see, the lame walk,
and prisoners leap forth in freedom.
All praise and glory be yours
through Christ and the Holy Spirit
forever and ever. Amen.

Psalm 118

The heathens encircled me;
in the name of Yahweh I destroyed them.
They swarmed round me closer and closer;
in the name of Yahweh I destroyed them.
They swarmed round me like bees;
they flamed like a fire of thorns.
In the name of Yahweh I destroyed them.
I was hard pressed, about to fall,
but Yahweh came to my help—
Yahweh you are my strength and my courage.
Yahweh, you have been my savior.
Let shouts of joy and victory ring out
in the tents of the righteous;
Yahweh's right hand has done mighty things.
Yahweh's right hand is lifted high.

Yahweh's right hand has done mighty things.
I shall not die, but live
to proclaim the deeds of Yahweh.
Though Yahweh has chastised me,
I am not abandoned to death.

(Vv. 10–18)

As we walk in the light of the Resurrection, we acclaim
the Author of Life, as we pray: *Faithful God, may your
name be praised in joy.*
- We give thanks to God for the gift of salvation, as we
  pray . . .
- We rejoice in God for the blessings of this season, as
  we pray . . .
- We celebrate our God, who has destroyed the sting of
  death, as we pray . . .
- We give thanks to God for Christ's being borne up to
  the right hand of glory, as we pray . . .
- (Other spontaneous prayers of petition or praise) . . .

Praise

God of all providence, we give you praise and thanks for
the free gift of our salvation in Christ. By the power of
the Resurrection, may your will be our peace. We ask
this through Christ our brother. Amen.

Closing

EVENING

Living God,
we give you thanks and praise
for the blessings bestowed upon us by your grace.
As daylight fades from our sight,
our eyes are enlightened
by the brilliance of the Risen One,
who is forever the light of humankind.
Inspired by the witness of Christians gone before us,
we walk by faith in you,
and our hearts are on fire.
You are always with us
to lead and sustain us on our journey.
All praise and thanks be yours
through Christ and the Holy Spirit
forever and ever. Amen.

Thanksgiving

Psalm 114 | Alleluia!
When Israel came forth from Egypt,
from a foreign nation,
Judah became God's temple;
Israel became God's kingdom.
The sea fled at the sight;
the Jordan reversed its course.
The mountains leapt like rams,
and the hills like lambs.
Why was it, sea, that you fled?
Jordan, why reverse your course?
Mountains, why leap like rams;
hills, like lambs?
Tremble, O earth, before Yahweh,
in the presence of God
who turns the rock into a pool
and flint into a spring of water.

Intercessions | Confident that God hears us, we offer our needs to the Creator, as we pray: *In your will we find our peace.*
- For the church, that we may be faithful to the journey of faith, let us pray . . .
- For the nations, that the peace of the Risen Christ may reign in the hearts and actions of all people, let us pray . . .
- For our community, that like the disciples on the road to Emmaus, we may recognize the Risen One in our midst, let us pray . . .
- For those held in chains of poverty, ignorance, addiction, or illness, that the power of the Risen Christ may set them free, let us pray . . .
- For the dead, that they may know the blessings of eternal life, let us pray . . .
- (Other spontaneous prayers of intercession or contrition, or an examination of conscience) . . .

Closing | God of all providence, we give you praise and thanks for the free gift of our salvation in Christ. By the power of the Resurrection, may your will be our peace. We ask this through Christ our brother. Amen.

Easter Tuesdays
Outside the Octave

Blessings and honor be yours,
Font of Everlasting Life.
As daylight scatters the darkness of night,
we gather to praise you
for the mystery of Christ's rising
that has brought us the fullness of your mercy.
Your justice and mercy
leave us awestruck and thankful.
The light of Christ shines in our hearts,
and so we raise our voices to praise you.
All honor and glory be yours
through Christ and the Holy Spirit
forever and ever. Amen.

Adoration

Open the gates of justice to me.
I will come in and give thanks to you, Yahweh.
This is Yahweh's gateway,
through which the righteous may enter.
I thank you for having heard me;
you have been my savior.
The stone rejected by the builders
has become the cornerstone;
this is Yahweh's doing,
and it is marvelous to see.
This is the day made memorable by Yahweh.
Let us rejoice and be glad.

(Vv. 19–24)

Psalm 118

Praise | This day is a gift from God. In joy we acclaim the Author of Life, as we pray: *Praise to you, Source of Peace.*
- We adore God, who has brought us the fullness of mercy, as we pray . . .
- We give thanks to God, who has ransomed us from the sting of death, as we pray . . .
- We honor the memory of the Crucified One, who is our joy, as we pray . . .
- We are filled with wonder at the bright promise of immortality, as we pray . . .
- (Other spontaneous prayers of petition or praise) . . .

Closing | Merciful and gracious God, we offer praise to you for the life that is ours in the Risen Jesus. Send us your spirit that we may always live in your love. We ask this through Christ our shepherd. Amen.

EVENING

Thanksgiving | Guardian of all creatures great and small,
we give you thanks and praise
as daylight draws to a close.
From sunrise to sunset your name is praised
by those who live by your call to love.
Christ Jesus is the light who guides us onward
and he who heals our wounded hearts.
Bathed in the light of Christ,
our hearts do not fear.
Our voices are raised with all the hosts of heaven
to give you thanks for the victory of the Lamb.
All praise and thanks be yours
through Christ and the Holy Spirit
forever and ever. Amen.

Psalm 91 | You who dwell in the shelter of the Most High,
who abide in the shadow of the Almighty,
say: "My Refuge and my Strength,
my God in whom I trust."
For God will save you from the snare of the fowler,
from the destroying pestilence.
With pinions God will cover you,
and under God's wings you shall find refuge;

God's faithfulness is a guard and a shield.
You will not fear the terror of the night
nor the arrow that flies by day;
not the pestilence that stalks in darkness
nor the plague that destroys at noon.
Though a thousand fall at your side,
ten thousand at your right side,
you will remain secure.
Behold, look with your own eyes
and see the punishment of the wicked—
because you have God for your refuge
You have made the Most High your stronghold.

(Vv. 1–9)

Intercessions

As the sun fades from our view, we bring the needs of
our weary earth to God the creator, as we pray: *May
your mercy rest on us.*

- For all Christians and for those recently received in
  baptism, let us pray . . .
- For the nations, that the peace of Christ may be the
  foundation of our common life, let us pray . . .
- For our community, in thanksgiving for all those
  whose generosity gives us the freedom to proclaim the
  Gospel, let us pray . . .
- For all those whose lives are shadowed in fear, that
  God may set them free, let us pray . . .
- For the dead, that they may be bathed in the light
  and rest of heaven, let us pray . . .
- (Other spontaneous prayers of intercession or contri-
  tion, or an examination of conscience) . . .

Closing

Merciful and gracious God, we offer praise to you for
the life that is ours in the Risen Jesus. Send us your
Spirit that we may always live in your love. We ask this
through Christ our shepherd. Amen.

Easter Wednesdays Outside the Octave

MORNING

Adoration

Blessed are you, Source of All Peace,
for the dawn of your love, which breaks upon us.
In this holy season,
we rejoice at the victory of Christ,
and our hearts offer a hymn of glory to you.
As daylight breaks upon us,
the earth thrills at your goodness.
All glory and praise be yours
through Christ and the Holy Spirit
forever and ever. Amen.

Psalm 118

Yahweh, please save us.
Yahweh, please help us prosper.
Blessings on the one who comes in the name of
　　　Yahweh!
We bless you from the house of Yahweh.
Yahweh is God and has made light to shine on us.
With branches in your hands, form the procession
as far as the corners of the altar.
You are my God, I give you thanks.
I celebrate you, my God;
I give you thanks for having heard me.
You have been my savior.
I give you thanks, Yahweh, for you are good;
your love is everlasting!

(Vv. 25–29)

Praise

We enter into the gift of this day of Resurrection, as we
pray: *God of peace, all praise be yours.*
- We adore our God whose radiance shines in the
  resurrection of Christ, as we pray . . .

- We give thanks to God for the unfathomable mystery of our salvation, as we pray . . .
- We rejoice in God for our conversion in Christ Jesus, as we pray . . .
- We proclaim our wonder at God's love for us poured out in the blood of Christ, as we pray . . .
- (Other spontaneous prayers of petition or praise) . . .

Closing

Almighty God, we celebrate the fullness of your love and justice, and we are bathed in the precious gift of your healing. Keep us mindful of the Gospel and, through the power of your spirit, strengthen us to proclaim the Resurrection to the ends of the earth. We ask this through Christ our hope. Amen.

EVENING

Thanksgiving

All praise and thanks to you, living God,
for the light of Christ,
which is your gift and our hope.
Through all the ages,
your praises have been sung
by those who trust
in the bright promise of your providence.
As daylight fades,
we place our fears at the feet of the Risen Jesus,
who has taken the orphans of this world
and made them your daughters and sons.
All praise and thanks be yours
through Christ and the Holy Spirit
forever and ever. Amen.

Psalm 144

Blessed be you, O God, my Rock,
who trains my hands for battle,
my arms for struggle;
my Refuge and my Fortress,
my Stronghold, my Deliverer,
my Shield in whom I trust.
God, what are we, that you care for us
or even take thought of us?
We are like a breath,
our days, like a passing shadow.

Part your heavens, O God, and come down;
touch the mountains and they shall smoke.
Send forth lightning, and put them to flight;
shoot your arrows and rout them.
Reach out your hand from on high—
rescue me from the mighty waters,
from the hands of strangers,
whose mouths swear false promises
while their right hands are raised in perjury.
O God, I will sing a new song to you;
with a ten-stringed lyre I will sing your praise—
you who give victory to rulers
and deliver David, your servant.

(Vv. 1–10)

Intercessions   In the shades of eventide, we present our needs to the living God, as we pray: *God of justice, hear our prayer.*

• For all Christians and for those recently baptized, that we may be faithful to our calling, let us pray . . .
• For all the earth, that an end may come to hostilities between nations and within hearts, let us pray . . .
• For our community, that the blessing of this Easter season may descend upon us, let us pray . . .
• For sick and suffering people, that the Risen Christ may be their healing, let us pray . . .
• For the dead, that the Lamb of God may guide them to heaven, let us pray . . .
• (Other spontaneous prayers of intercession or contrition, or an examination of conscience) . . .

Closing   Almighty God, we celebrate the fullness of your love and justice, and we are bathed in the precious gift of your healing. Keep us mindful of the Gospel and, through the power of your spirit, strengthen us to proclaim the Resurrection to the ends of the earth. We ask this through Christ our hope. Amen.

Easter Thursdays
Outside the Octave

Glory to you, O God,
whose cords of love have bound us to one another.
From the side of the crucified Christ,
you have given birth to a priestly people.
Through the ages,
your church has sent forth the fragrance
of your eternal springtime
and proclaimed the end to the power of death
and the beginning of Christ's promise of immortality.
All praise and glory be yours
through Christ and the Holy Spirit
forever and ever. Amen.

Adoration

Praise God from the heavens;
praise God in the heights;
praise God, all you angels;
praise God, all you heavenly hosts.
Praise God, sun and moon;
praise God, all you shining stars.
Praise God, you highest heavens,
and you waters above the heavens.
Let them praise the name of God,
who commanded and they were created.
God established them forever and ever
and gave a decree which shall not pass away.
Be this God praised by all the faithful ones,
by the children of Israel, the people close to God.
Alleluia.

Psalm 148

(Vv. 1–6,14)

Praise | As we awaken to yet another day of Easter joy, we glorify God, as we pray: *God of life, may you be blessed.*
- We marvel at the inexpressible mystery of the Resurrection, as we pray . . .
- We are filled with awe at the mercy of God, as we pray . . .
- Our frail lives are strengthened in the gift of salvation, as we pray . . .
- All creation rejoices at the bright victory of the Risen Christ, as we pray . . .
- (Other spontaneous prayers of petition or praise) . . .

Closing | Tender and powerful God, we are filled with joy at the vision of the Risen Christ in our midst. Guide us always through this earthly pilgrimage until you raise us to the fullness of life. We ask this through Christ our way. Amen.

EVENING

Thanksgiving | All praise and thanks be yours,
God of all Creation.
As evening falls,
we remember the compassion and love
you poured out for us
in the blood of our Innocent Redeemer.
Calling us to unity of mind and heart in you,
Jesus faithfully proclaimed your Word
and gave a new message of life and peace to us.
The presence of Christ among us
is an eternal lamp,
guiding us to your resplendent day.
All praise and thanks be yours
through Christ and the Holy Spirit
forever and ever. Amen.

Psalm 147 | Praise God, who is good;
sing praise to our God, who is gracious.
It is fitting to praise God.
God rebuilds Jerusalem,
gathers the exiles of Israel.

God heals the brokenhearted
and binds up all their wounds.
God knows the number of the stars
and calls them each by name.
Great is our God and mighty in power;
there is no limit to God's wisdom.
Yahweh sustains the lowly
and casts the wicked to the ground.
Sing to God with thanksgiving;
sing praise with the harp to our God,
who covers the heavens with clouds,
who provides rain for the earth,
and who makes grass grow on the mountains,
who gives food to the cattle,
and to the young ravens when they call.
God does not delight in the strength of the steed,
nor is God pleased with the fleetness of humans.
God is pleased with those who have reverence,
with those who hope in faithful love.

(Vv. 1–11)

Intercessions

Daylight draws to a close, yet our hearts are filled with
hope. Therefore we bring our needs to God, as we pray:
God, have mercy on your people.

- For the People of God, especially those reborn this
  season in baptism, that the gift of the Resurrection
  may be our life, let us pray . . .
- For people of every race and tongue, that the light of
  Christ may guide our way to peace, let us pray . . .
- For our community, that the peace of this season may
  nourish us every day of our lives, let us pray . . .
- For those whose lives are marred by violence and
  oppression, that the blood of the Lamb may be their
  anointing and their hope, let us pray . . .
- For all those who have died, especially those who
  have died this day in loneliness, let us pray . . .
- (Other spontaneous prayers of intercession or contrition, or an examination of conscience) . . .

Closing | Tender and powerful God, we are filled with joy at the vision of the Risen Christ in our midst. Guide us always through this earthly pilgrimage until you raise us to the fullness of life. We ask this through Christ our way. Amen.

Easter Fridays
Outside the Octave

God of all life,
we give you heartfelt praise as daylight dawns.
This day we are filled with joy
for the sign of your immense love
raised up for us on the heights of Calvary.
When Jesus stretched forth his arms upon the cross,
you sealed for us
an eternal and unbreakable bond of love
for which the hearts of all people thirst.
All glory and praise be yours
through Christ and the Holy Spirit
forever and ever. Amen.

Adoration

Sing to Yahweh a new song of praise
in the assembly of the faithful.
Let Israel rejoice in their Maker;
let the people of Zion be glad in their God.
Let them praise God's name in a festive dance;
let them sing praise to God with timbrel and harp.
For God loves the people
and crowns the lowly with victory.
Let the faithful rejoice;
let them sing for joy upon their couches—
let the high praises of God be in their mouths.
And let two-edged swords be in their hands
to execute vengeance on the nations,
punishments on the peoples;
to bind their rulers with chains,
their nobles with fetters;
to execute on them the written sentence.

Psalm 149

This is the glory of all the faithful.
Alleluia.

Praise

Again the sun bathes us in the brilliance of the Risen Christ. With joy, we pray: *God of joy, all praise be yours.*
- We adore God, who gives us this day of salvation, as we pray . . .
- We give God thanks for conquering death, as we pray . . .
- We offer our praise to God who sent Christ to vanquish evil, as we pray . . .
- We are filled with joy for the presence of the Christ in our midst, as we pray . . .
- (Other spontaneous prayers of petition or praise) . . .

Closing

Author of Life, hear our prayer and keep us faithful to your will. As we journey through this season of the Resurrection, deepen our faith and move us to proclaim eternal life given in Christ. We ask this through Christ our good shepherd. Amen.

EVENING

Thanksgiving

Most blessed God,
we give you praise and thanks
as now the shades of evening descend upon us.
As lamps are kindled,
we recall the mystery of Christ's passion
and the obedience of Jesus to your will.
Jesus is the light of our salvation,
and we rejoice that Christ is our eternal mediator,
bearing us toward your mercy.
All praise and thanks be yours
through Christ and the Holy Spirit
forever and ever. Amen.

Psalm 146

Alleluia!
Praise Yahweh, O my soul!
I will praise you, Yahweh, all my life;
I will sing praise to you as long as I live.
Do not put your trust in rulers,
in humans in whom there is no salvation.

When their spirits depart they return to the earth;
on that very day their plans perish.
Happy those whose help is the God of Jacob and
    Rachel,
whose hope is in Yahweh, their God,
the Maker of heaven and earth,
the sea, and all that is in them;
who keeps faith forever,
secures justice for the oppressed,
and gives food to the hungry.
Yahweh, you set captives free
and give sight to the blind.
You raise up those that were bowed down
and love the just.
You protect strangers;
the orphan and the widow you sustain,
but the way of the wicked you thwart.
Yahweh shall reign forever—
your God, O Zion, through all generations. Alleluia.

Grateful for the cross and the resurrection of Christ, we offer our needs to God, as we pray: *Bless your people, God of love.*

- For all those who confess Jesus as the Messiah, that the Spirit may sustain us until the Second Coming, let us pray . . .
- For all the earth, that the compassion of the Risen Christ may be the inspiration of every leader and government, let us pray . . .
- For our community, that the spirit of this season may guide every thought, word, and deed, let us pray . . .
- For all those whose faith is sorely tried by compulsions or sin, that God may strengthen them until the day of their liberty, let us pray . . .
- For the dead, that together we may one day come to the brilliance of the Second Coming, let us pray . . .
- (Other spontaneous prayers of intercession or contrition, or an examination of conscience) . . .

Intercessions

Closing | Author of Life, hear our prayers and keep us faithful to your will. As we journey through this season of the Resurrection, deepen our faith and move us to proclaim Eternal Life to all the nations. We ask this through Christ our good shepherd. Amen.

Easter Saturdays
Outside the Octave

Adoration

God of light and peace, be praised.
As the rays of your love warm our weary hearts,
we are grateful
that we have fallen into the hands of your providence.
In life and in death we belong to you alone.
To you this day we raise our songs of joy
for the gift of the resurrection of Christ.
As you give to us this day of peace,
we proclaim that the light of Christ
is the source of all hope for the nations.
All glory and praise be yours
through Christ and the Holy Spirit
forever and ever. Amen.

Psalm 150

Alleluia!
Praise to you, Yahweh, in your sanctuary!
Praise to you in the firmament of your strength.
Praise you for your mighty deeds;
praise for your sovereign majesty.
Praise to you, Yahweh, with the blast of the trumpet,
praise with lyre and harp.
Praise with timbrel and dance;
praise with strings and flute.
Praise to you, Yahweh, with resounding cymbals;
praise with clanging cymbals.
Let everything that has breath praise Yahweh.
Alleluia.

Praise | This is God's day, and we are made glad. In joy, we proclaim: *Praise to you, God of life.*
- We adore God for our sanctification in the Risen Christ, as we pray . . .
- We give God thanks for the gift of those reborn this season in baptism, as we pray . . .
- We are filled with joy for the faith of the People of God, as we pray . . .
- We are filled with wonder at the suffering of Christ, which has changed our tears into joy, as we pray . . .
- (Other spontaneous prayers of petition or praise) . . .

Closing | Loving, compassionate God, you have redeemed us in the waters of baptism and have immersed us into the Body of Christ. As you sustained the Mother of Jesus in all fidelity to the Word, nourish us always until we come to the eternal Jerusalem. We ask this through Christ our brother. Amen.

The Ascension

God of all life,
we give you praise and thanks as daylight ends,
and we are brought to the beginning of night.
This day we celebrate the Ascension of Christ Jesus
and the birth of your people
to the glory of your love.
Jesus has borne us up on eagle's wings
to your right hand;
and all creation has entered into a new age
of your peace and justice.
Buoyed upon the wings of your liberty,
we sing your praise for the gift of Christ
whose light never fades.
All praise and thanks be yours
through Christ and the Holy Spirit
forever and ever. Amen.

Thanksgiving

Yahweh, I am calling. Hasten to me;
hear me—I am calling to you.
My prayers rise like incense,
my hands like the evening sacrifice.
Yahweh, set a guard at my mouth,
a watch at the door of my lips.
Do not let my heart be compelled to wrong doing,
to share in the deeds of the evildoers.
No, I will not taste their delights.
A just person may strike me in reproof—
it is a kindness;
such a rebuke is oil on my head!
My prayer is ever against the deeds of evildoers.

Psalm 141

To you, Yahweh, I turn my eyes.
In you I take shelter—
do not hand me over to death.
Keep me out of traps that are set for me,
from the bait laid for me by evil ones.

(Vv. 1–5,8–9)

Intercessions

On this festival of the Ascension, we bear our needs to Holy Providence, as we pray: *Loving God, receive our prayer*.

- For all Christians, that our gaze toward the living light may strengthen us until the last day, let us pray . . .
- For all the nations, that peoples of every age may thirst for the peace and justice of the reign of God, let us pray . . .
- For our community, that our service to one another may be a witness to the Gospel, let us pray . . .
- For suffering people and those who mourn, that the Divine Healer may bring them release and peace, let us pray . . .

- For all those who have died, that Jesus may raise them to glory, let us pray . . .
- (Other spontaneous prayers of intercession or contrition, or an examination of conscience) . . .

God, we adore you for the mystery of the Ascension of Jesus, who is forever our one and final mediator. Grant us your mercy in this life, that we may come to the fullness of your reign. We ask this through Christ our light. Amen.

Closing

MORNING

Adoration

Blessed are you, God of endless glory,
for the daylight that scatters the darkness of night.
Today Christ is brought to your right hand,
and all creation rejoices at the gift of redemption.
In glory, Jesus ascends to heaven,
bearing to you a redeemed and thankful people
made clean in the blood of the eternal Passover.
All glory and praise be yours
through Christ and the Holy Spirit
forever and ever. Amen.

I thank you, Yahweh, with all my heart;
I sing praise to you before the angels.
I worship at your holy temple and praise your name
because of your constant love and faithfulness,
because you have shown that you and your word are
    exalted.
You answered me when I called to you;
you built up strength within me.
All the rulers of the earth will praise you, Yahweh,
because they have heard your promises.
They will sing about your ways
and about your great glory.
Even though you are exalted,
you care for the lowly.
The proud cannot hide from you.
Even when I am surrounded by troubles,
you keep me safe;

Psalm 138

you oppose my angry enemies
and save me by your power.
You will do everything you have promised me;
Yahweh, your faithful love endures forever.
Complete the work that you have begun.

Praise Jesus the Christ has ascended, and so we acclaim the greatness of God, as we pray: *Glory to God in the highest.*
- We rejoice at the Ascension of Jesus, as we pray . . .
- We are filled with wonder at the bright promise of immortality, as we pray . . .
- We are awed at the unfathomable love of God, as we pray . . .
- We are grateful for God's infinite mercy towards humankind, as we pray . . .
- (Other spontaneous prayers of petition or praise) . . .

Closing God, we adore you for the mystery of the Ascension of Jesus, who is forever our one and final mediator. Grant us your mercy in this life, that we may come to the fullness of your reign. We ask this through Christ our light. Amen.

Pentecost

Thanksgiving

All praise and thanks be yours, eternal God,
for the light of Christ,
which scatters the darkness from among us.
This day your Holy Spirit
has descended upon us.
The curse of Babel's confusion
has been shattered.
Your church has come to birth,
and all people can hear the eloquence
of your justice and peace.
No longer timid before the shades of death,
your truth is a symphony to all believers.
Your spirit brings hope to all the world.
All praise and thanks be yours
through Christ and the Holy Spirit
forever and ever. Amen.

Psalm 113

Alleluia!
Praise, you servants of Yahweh,
praise the name of Yahweh!
May Yahweh's name be blessed
both now and forever!
From east to west, from north to south,
praised be the name of Yahweh!
High above all nations, Yahweh!
Your glory transcends the heavens!
Who is like you, Yahweh our God?
Enthroned so high, you have to stoop
to see the heavens and earth!

You raise the poor from the dust
and lift the needy from the dunghill
to give them a place with rulers,
with the nobles of your people.
Yahweh, you give the barren a home,
making them glad with children.

Intercessions | Strengthened by the power of the Spirit, we lay our needs before God, as we pray: *Living God, renew us in your love.*

- For all Christians, that the winds of a new Pentecost may move us to deeds of peace and justice, let us pray . . .
- For all those who nourish us in faith, that the Spirit of prudence and wisdom may be sown in their lives, let us pray . . .
- For our community, that the Spirit of ardent love may inflame us to a greater service of one another, let us pray . . .
- For all those constrained by addiction, ignorance, fear, or illness, that the Holy Spirit may bring liberation and healing, let us pray . . .
- For the dead, that the light of Christ may guide them on their journey to the joys of heaven, let us pray . . .
- (Other spontaneous prayers of intercession or contrition, or an examination of conscience) . . .

Closing | Loving and gracious God, today the fire of your Holy Spirit enkindles the face of the earth. May the warmth of Christ's presence among us give us the strength to speak your wisdom and the power to accomplish your will. We ask this through Christ our strength and counsel. Amen.

MORNING

Thanksgiving | Blessed are you, God of all creation.
At the dawn of time,
your spirit hovered over the waters
and brought into being all that lives.
After Christ returned to you in glory,

your spirit descended upon the disciples
and, with a mighty wind,
shook the place where they were,
making them courageous witnesses of the Gospel.
This day your spirit hovers over your people
making us bold to speak your goodness
to the very ends of the earth.
All praise and glory be yours
through Christ and the Holy Spirit
forever and ever. Amen.

Alleluia! **Psalm 150**
Praise to you, Yahweh, in your sanctuary!
Praise to you in the firmament of your strength.
Praise you for your mighty deeds;
praise you for your sovereign majesty.
Praise to you, Yahweh, with the blast of the trumpet,
praise with lyre and harp.
Praise with timbrel and dance;
praise with strings and flute.
Praise to you, Yahweh, with resounding cymbals;
praise with clanging cymbals.
Let everything that has breath praise Yahweh.
Alleluia.

As the Spirit of God calls us to the dawn of a new **Praise**
creation, let us cry out in joy: *Honor and praise be yours,*
O Living God.
- We are filled with joy at the anointing of the Spirit
  upon us, as we pray . . .
- We offer God thanks for the gift of the Spirit who
  heals us in mind and heart, as we pray . . .
- We are filled with wonder at the fire of the Spirit,
  which moves us to charity, as we pray . . .
- We are awed by the presence of the Spirit that calls
  us to peacemaking, as we pray . . .
- (Other spontaneous prayers of petition or praise) . . .

Closing | Loving and gracious God, today the fire of your Holy Spirit enkindles the face of the earth. May the warmth of Christ's presence among us give us the strength to speak your wisdom and the power to accomplish your will. We ask this through Christ our strength and counsel. Amen.

Special Needs

Christian Unity

Adoration

All praise and honor to you, one true God,
for the gift of your Word,
which is the salvation and unity of the whole world.
At the beginning of time, you spoke
and the waters gave birth
to all that lives and breathes.
In the fullness of time,
your Word became flesh in the womb of Mary,
the image of your church.
Your Word called the first disciples of Jesus
to holiness of heart, unity of life,
and charity in service.
We praise you for all women and men, united in faith,
who announce your salvation from sunrise to sunset
to the many nations of earth.
All praise and honor be to you
through Christ and the Holy Spirit
forever and ever. Amen.

Psalm 63

O God, you are my God whom I eagerly seek;
for you my flesh longs and my soul thirsts
like the earth, parched, lifeless, and without water.
I have gazed toward you in the sanctuary
to see your power and your glory.
For your love is better than life;
my lips shall glorify you.
Thus will I praise you while I live;
lifting up my hands, I will call upon your name.
As with the riches of a banquet shall my soul be filled,
and with exultant lips my mouth shall praise you.

On my bed I will remember you,
and through the night watches I will meditate on you:
because you are my help,
and in the shadow of your wings I shout for joy.
My soul clings to you;
your right hand upholds me

(Vv. 1–8)

Praise

This day we celebrate one faith and one baptism in Christ. In joy we pray: *Honor and praise are yours, God of compassion.*

- We glorify God, who has spoken the Word of unity to all the nations, as we pray . . .
- We give thanks and praise for all those who call the church to unity and peace, as we pray . . .
- We are filled with wonder at the power of the Word that heals and reconciles us, as we pray . . .
- We are thankful for Jesus, living in our midst, who moves us to be of one mind and one heart, as we pray . . .
- (Other spontaneous prayers of petition or praise) . . .

Closing

Living God, you send your spirit to unite us in the covenant of love. As we confess sorrow for the divisions among us, we know that it is your spirit that can bind us into the unity of the one Body of Christ. Continue to nourish us until that day when we shall be united and come to the one feast of your eternal peace. We ask this through Christ our hope of unity. Amen.

EVENING

Thanksgiving

Eternal God of all creation,
we give you thanks and praise
for the wonders of your love.
Your Word has called us to be a new creation.
Your Spirit has freed us from the ancient curse,
which scattered the nations in confusion.
Jesus, your Christ, is the eternal lamp,
kindled in our midst, dispelling darkness
and calling us to be of one mind and one heart in you.

When the hour of that first Easter night had come,
Christ breathed the Spirit of peace upon the gathered
    disciples
so that they might proclaim to all the world
the unity of the church, the Body of Christ.
This night we gather as one people
looking forward to the final day of your justice.
All praise and thanks to you
through Christ and the Holy Spirit
forever and ever. Amen.

Psalm 133

How good it is, how pleasant,
for God's people to live in unity.
It is like the precious oil
running down from Aaron's head and beard,
down to the collar of his robes.
It is like the dew on Mount Hermon
falling on the hills of Zion.
For there Yahweh has promised a blessing,
life that never ends.

Intercessions

As we are gathered in the hope of the unity of all Christians, let us offer our needs to our God, as we pray: *Keep us mindful of your love.*

- For all the Christian church, that our vision of the reign of God may bind us in unity, let us pray . . .
- For all ministers of the Word, that their proclamation may call us to a new unity of mind and heart, let us pray . . .
- For our community, that our life and worship may contribute to the unity of the Body of Christ, let us pray . . .
- For all those who suffer from loneliness and despair, that God may grant them the gift of sincere human communion, let us pray . . .
- For the dead, that their entrance into the communion of heaven may move us to deeds of unity and peace, let us pray . . .
- (Other spontaneous prayers of intercession or contrition, or an examination of conscience) . . .

Almighty God, you call us to the covenant of love. As we confess sorrow for the divisions among us, we know that it is your spirit that can bind us into the unity of the one Body of Christ. Continue to nourish us until that day when we shall be united and come to the one feast of your eternal peace. We ask this through Christ our source of unity. Amen.

Closing

Mary, Mother of Jesus the Christ

Adoration

Praise to you, loving God, as daylight dawns
for the gift of Christ
whose resurrection is the hope of the world.
In Jesus, your people have been brought
to the fullness of your grace.
This day we honor the memory of the woman
whose fidelity to your Word
enriches our spiritual journey.
As she brought the Word to birth in her life,
so you give her to us
as an image of discipleship in grace.
All praise and honor be yours,
through Christ and the Holy Spirit
forever and ever. Amen.

Psalm 147

Glorify Yahweh, O Jerusalem;
praise your God, O Zion.
For God has strengthened the bars of your gates
and has blessed your children within you.
God has granted peace on your borders
and fills you with the best of wheat.
God sends forth a command to the earth;
swiftly runs the word!
God spreads snow like wool
and scatters frost like ashes.
God scatters hail like crumbs;
before God's cold, the waters freeze.
God sends a word and melts them;
God lets the breeze blow and the waters flow.
God's word has been proclaimed to Jacob,
laws and decrees to Israel.

God has not done this for any other nation;
God has not made such laws known to them. Alleluia.
(Vv. 12–20)

Praise

As we honor Mary, we praise the God of salvation, as we pray: *We lift our minds and hearts to you, loving and merciful God.*
• We praise you, God, for the wonders of your love, as we pray . . .
• We praise the holy name of God planted in our hearts, as we pray . . .
• We rejoice in the fidelity of Mary to the living Word of God, as we pray . . .
• We celebrate with joy our own birth in Christ, as we pray . . .
• (Other spontaneous prayers of petition or praise) . . .

Closing

Loving God, we celebrate and honor Mary, the mother of our savior, Jesus Christ. Grant us the gift of your spirit, that we may, like Mary, bring the presence of the Word to birth in our words and deeds of love. We ask this through Christ our brother. Amen.

EVENING

Thanksgiving

Loving and faithful God,
we give you thanks and praise for Jesus,
the source of peace and light of the world,
blazing forth in our midst this night.
As the shades of evening gather,
we offer to you our sacrifice of praise
for the presence of Christ,
who alone has restored us to Eden's innocence.
With joy, we join the Mother of Christ
in echoing the song of your promise:
poor people are enriched, hungry people have their fill,
and lowly people are raised to new heights.
All praise and thanks be yours
through Christ and the Holy Spirit
forever and ever. Amen.

Psalm 45

My heart overflows with a goodly theme;
I address my verses to the king;
my tongue is like the pen of a ready scribe.
You are the fairest of all;
grace is poured upon your lips;
thus God has blessed you forever.
Gird your sword upon your side, O mighty one,
clothe yourself with glory and majesty!
Hear, O daughter, consider, and turn your ear;
forget your people and your ancestor's home.
The king will desire your beauty.
The people of Tyre are here with gifts,
the richest of the people seeking your favor.
The place of your ancestors your children shall have;
you will make them rulers through all the earth.
I will cause your name to be celebrated in all generations;
therefore the peoples will praise you forever and ever.

(Vv. 1–3,10–12,16–17)

Intercessions

As we come to night's beginning, we offer our needs to
God who looked upon Mary in her lowliness, as we pray:
Keep us mindful of your love.

- For the church throughout the world, that like Mary,
  we may be faithful to the service of the Word, let us
  pray . . .
- For those who lead us in faith and government, that
  they may be inspired by the Word, which lifts downtrodden people, let us pray . . .
- For our community, that the example of Mary's embrace of God's will may be a leaven for our life and
  service, let us pray . . .
- For poor, lowly, and oppressed people, that the freedom and dignity of the Gospel may raise them up, let
  us pray . . .
- (Other spontaneous prayers of intercession or contrition, or an examination of conscience) . . .

Closing

Loving God, we celebrate and honor Mary, the mother
of our savior, Jesus Christ. Grant us the gift of your
spirit, that like Mary, we may bring the presence of the
Word to birth in our words and deeds of love. We ask
this through Christ our brother. Amen.

Joseph

Blessed are you, Holy One.
From the dawn of creation,
you offered a covenant of love to sinful humanity.
With Abraham and Sarah, all earth rejoices
that you have given us the fullness of salvation
in Jesus, our Messiah, the Word of Life.
Born into poverty,
Jesus was tenderly embraced in justice and love
by Mary and Joseph.
Today, we celebrate the memory of that man,
whose dedication to your Word,
the Fountain of Life itself,
inspires our labor to build your reign.
All praise and honor be yours
through Christ and the Holy Spirit
forever and ever. Amen.

Adoration

God, show your faithfulness, bless us,
and make your face smile on us!
For then the earth will acknowledge your ways,
and all the nations will know of your power to save.
May all the nations praise you, O God;
may all the nations praise you!
Let the nations shout and sing for joy
since you dispense true justice to the world.
You grant strict justice to the peoples;
on earth you guide the nations.
Let the nations praise you, God;
let all the nations praise you!
The soil has given its harvest;
God, our God, has blessed us.
May God continue to bless us;
and let God be feared to the very ends of the earth.

Psalm 67

Praise With Joseph and all the saints, we offer our adoration to God, as we pray: *Honor and praise are yours, God of love and justice.*

- We give thanks to God for our salvation in Christ, as we pray . . .
- We stand in awe of the mercy of God, as we pray . . .
- We are grateful to God for sending us Jesus the Messiah, protected and instructed by Joseph, the carpenter, so we pray . . .
- We praise God for the gift of love, which is our peace, as we pray . . .
- (Other spontaneous prayers of petition or praise) . . .

Closing God, you gave the care of Jesus to Joseph. Just as Joseph embraced Jesus in love, may we also embrace Jesus. We ask this through Christ our brother. Amen.

EVENING

Thanksgiving God of glory,
we give you praise and thanks for the gift of Jesus,
the light of all the world.
From ancient days, you yearned to bring creation
from the darkness of fear into the light of your peace.
In every age,
you raise up those who herald to all the world
the brilliance of your goodness.
Joseph, the just man, in the silence of his heart,
adored you and nourished the Word of life
in Jesus, our Messiah.
As justice blossomed in his life,
so it has flowered in the bosom of the church
as a sign of your presence to us in Christ.
All praise and thanks be yours
through Christ and the Holy Spirit
forever and ever. Amen.

Psalm 141 Yahweh, I am calling. Hasten to me;
hear me—I am calling to you.
My prayers rise like incense,
my hands like the evening sacrifice.

Yahweh, set a guard at my mouth,
a watch at the door of my lips.
Do not let my heart be compelled to wrong doing,
to share in the deeds of the evildoers.
No, I will not taste their delights.
A just person may strike me in reproof—
it is a kindness;
such a rebuke is oil on my head!
My prayer is ever against the deeds of evildoers.
To you, Yahweh, I turn my eyes.
In you I take shelter—
do not hand me over to death.
Keep me out of traps that are set for me,
from the bait laid for me by evil ones.

(Vv. 1–5,8–9)

Intercessions

As we honor the memory of Joseph and rejoice in his companionship, we offer our needs to God, as we pray: *Keep us mindful of your love.*

- For the church, that like Joseph, we may be faithful to the service of the Word, let us pray . . .
- For all the nations, that the search for peace may lead us to deeds of justice, let us pray . . .
- For our community, that in our labor the silent presence of the Word of life may be made manifest, let us pray . . .
- For those whose lives are scarred by emptiness, confusion, or doubt, that the Spirit may lead them to true peace, let us pray . . .
- For those who have died, that they may dwell in the joy and peace of heaven, let us pray . . .
- (Other spontaneous prayers of intercession or contrition, or an examination of conscience) . . .

Closing

God, you gave the care of Jesus to Joseph. Just as Joseph embraced Jesus in love, may we also embrace Jesus. We ask this through Christ our brother. Amen.

The Lives of Saints

Adoration

Praise to you, source of all holiness,
for sending the Christ
in whose blood we have been redeemed
and brought to the bright promise
of your eternal banquet.
From the pierced side of Jesus,
you washed your holy people in sanctity.
In every age,
women and men proclaim your gift of salvation.
Through the example of your holy ones,
you remind us of the destiny
to which all creation has been called.
In Christ, the voices of your saints
are joined with all creation to give you praise.
All glory and honor be yours
through Christ and the Holy Spirit
forever and ever. Amen.

Psalm 24

The world and all that is in it belong to Yahweh,
the earth and all who live on it.
Yahweh built it on the deep waters,
laid its foundations in the oceans' depths.
Who has the right to climb Yahweh's mountain?
Or stand in this holy place?
Those who are pure in act and in thought,
who do not worship idols
or make false promises.
Yahweh will bless them.
God their Savior will give them salvation.
Such are the people who come to God,
who come into the presence of our God.

(Vv. 1–6)

With the chorus of all the saints, we offer to God our morning sacrifice of praise, as we pray: *Holy God, we praise your name.*

- We praise God, who calls all people to holiness, as we pray . . .
- We worship our Creator, who calls all people to peace, as we pray . . .
- We honor the Source of All Life, who has brought us to redemption, as we pray . . .
- We give thanks to God for the companionship and example of all the saints, as we pray . . .
- (Other spontaneous prayers of petition or praise) . . .

Praise

Merciful God, we remember this day the lives of all the saints and are grateful for their example of love and service. Through the power of your Holy Spirit, bring us through our journey of life until the day when every nation shall feast upon your holy mountain in tranquility and joy. We ask this through Christ our savior. Amen.

Closing

EVENING

God of all justice,
as the shades of evening descend upon us,
we give you praise and thanks
for your free gift of redemption,
which has come to us in Christ Jesus.
In Christ you have brought all creation
from the darkness of sin
to the brightness of true liberty and holiness.
We give you thanks for the witness of your saints,
whose lives proclaim the light of Christ
to every people and nation.
We stand in the promise of your spirit
that continues to call us
to the same holiness of life.
All praise and thanks be yours
through Christ and the Holy Spirit
forever and ever. Amen.

Thanksgiving

Sing to Yahweh a new song of praise
in the assembly of the faithful.
Let Israel rejoice in their Maker;

Psalm 149

let the people of Zion be glad in their God.
Let them praise God's name in a festive dance;
let them sing praise to God with timbrel and harp.
For God loves the people
and crowns the lowly with victory.
Let the faithful rejoice;
let them sing for joy upon their couches—
let the high praises of God be in their mouths.
And let two-edged swords be in their hands
to execute vengeance on the nations,
punishments on the peoples;
to bind their rulers with chains,
their nobles with fetters;
to execute on them the written sentence.
This is the glory of all the faithful.
Alleluia.

Intercessions

In the memory of the saints, let us offer our needs to God as we pray: *Gracious God, keep us mindful of your love.*

- For the church, that we may ever be faithful to the gift of holiness, let us pray . . .
- For the gifts of justice and peace, that the Lamb of God may bring all peoples to conversion of life, let us pray . . .
- For our community, that we may welcome the stranger, the orphan, and the widowed into our midst, let us pray . . .
- For suffering people and all those who are in chains, that following the example of the saints, we may be instruments of God's liberation, let us pray . . .
- For all those who have died, that their companionship may nourish us as we journey, let us pray . . .
- (Other spontaneous prayers of intercession or contrition, or an examination of conscience) . . .

Closing

Merciful God, we remember this day the lives of all the saints and are grateful for their example of love and service. Through the power of your Holy Spirit, bring us through our journey of life until the day when every nation shall feast upon your holy mountain in tranquility and joy. We ask this through Christ our savior. Amen.

Justice and Peace

Glory to you, God of justice and peace,
for sending Jesus the Christ,
who teaches us how
to live peacefully and walk justly.
In him, we know the ultimate victory of
justice over injustice, and peace over war.
All praise and honor be yours
through Christ and the Holy Spirit
forever and ever. Amen.

Adoration

Fret not because of the wicked;
be not envious of wrongdoers!
For they will soon fade like the grass
and wither like the green herb.
Trust in Yahweh and do good
so you will dwell in the land and enjoy security.
The wicked draw their swords and bend their bows
to bring down the poor and the needy,
to slay those whose ways are upright.
Their swords shall enter their own hearts,
and their bows shall all be broken.
Better is the little that the just have
than the abundance of the wicked;
for the arms of the wicked shall be broken,
but Yahweh upholds the just.
. . . God delights in the way of the virtuous.
Though falling, they shall not be cast headlong,
for the hand of Yahweh supports them.

(Vv. 1–3,14–17,23–24)

Psalm 37

Jesus calls us to be people of justice and peace. We praise
God for sending the perfect peacemaker to serve as our

Praise

185

model and redeemer. And we pray: *God, make us instruments of your peace and justice.*

- We thank you, God, for sending Jesus, the shepherd of our souls, into our midst to lead us to your peace, and we pray . . .
- We desire to have faith that ultimately justice will conquer injustice and that peace will vanquish war, and we pray . . .
- We celebrate Jesus, our hope, who shows us that death is overcome by love, and we pray . . .
- We praise you for showing us how to love, to act justly, and to heal our wounded world through Jesus, and we pray . . .
- (Other spontaneous prayers of petition or praise) . . .

Closing | Just and loving God, we are grateful for the example of Jesus, who shows us that peace is more powerful than hate and justice is more lasting than injustice. Like the prophets and Jesus, modern martyrs teach us to be people of peace and bringers of justice. We honor them in our words and ask for grace to honor them more fully in our actions. May we come, through the power of the Holy Spirit, to make of our lives a sign of your peace for all the world. We ask this through Christ our salvation. Amen.

EVENING

Thanksgiving | We give you thanks and praise, patient and kind God, for all acts of compassion and deeds of justice.
Jesus preached the Good News
that hungry people should be fed,
sick people healed,
imprisoned people visited, and
ignorant people taught.
He called us to steward the land,
make peace with our neighbor,
and judge fairly in disputes.
In Jesus is hope and joy,
celebration and song.
All thanks and praise be yours
through Christ and the Holy Spirit
forever and ever. Amen.

When God brought back the captives of Zion,
we were like those who dream.
Then our mouths were filled with laughter
and our tongues with rejoicing;
then they said among the nations,
"Yahweh has done great things for them."
Yahweh has done great things for us;
we are truly glad.
Restore our fortunes, Yahweh,
like the streams in the Negeb!
May those who sow in tears
reap with songs of joy!
Those that go forth weeping,
carrying seed for the sowing,
shall come home with shouts of joy,
bringing the sheaves with them.

Psalm 126

As we celebrate the witness of those whose lives burn
for justice and peace, we offer our needs to God, as we
pray: *Keep us mindful of your love.*
- For all those who exercise authority in faith or in
  government, that their service may be inspired by the
  Good Shepherd, let us pray . . .
- For our community, that mutual charity may be the
  sign of justice and peace in our midst, let us pray . . .
- For those living with sickness, hatred, or oppression,
  that the passion of Christ may strengthen them and
  move us to their service, let us pray . . .
- For those who rest now in Christ, let us pray . . .
- (Other spontaneous prayers of intercession or contrition, or an examination of conscience) . . .

Intercessions

Just and loving God, we are grateful for the example of
Jesus, who shows us that peace is more powerful than
hate and justice is more lasting than injustice. Like the
prophets and Jesus, modern martyrs teach us to be
people of peace and bringers of justice. We honor them
in our words and ask for grace to honor them more fully
in our actions. May we come, through the power of the
Holy Spirit, to make of our lives a sign of your peace for
all the world. We ask this through Christ our salvation.
Amen.

Closing

The Faithful Departed

Adoration

Living God,
whose dawn has broken the chains of death,
we give you praise and thanks for the gift of life.
From the day when we first spurned your love,
we condemned ourselves to the power of evil.
Your mercy could never abandon us.
With the death and resurrection of Christ,
you saved us
and brought us to a new day of immortality.
This day we celebrate with the faithful departed
that the sting of death is no more
and that the bright dawn of eternal life
is your promise and our hope.
We give you praise for all those
who have passed from this life
and rest now in your peace.
With them as our companions in the faith,
we give you praise and honor
through Christ and the Holy Spirit
forever and ever. Amen.

Psalm 146

Alleluia!
Praise Yahweh, O my soul!
I will praise, you, Yahweh, all my life;
I will sing praise to you as long as I live.
Do not put your trust in rulers,
in humans in whom there is no salvation.
When their spirits depart they return to the earth;
on that very day their plans perish.
Happy those whose help is the God of Jacob and Rachel,
whose hope is in Yahweh, their God,
the Maker of heaven and earth,
the sea, and all that is in them;

who keeps faith forever,
secures justice for the oppressed,
and gives food to the hungry.
Yahweh, you set captives free
and give sight to the blind.
You raise up those that were bowed down
and love the just.
You protect strangers;
the orphan and the widow you sustain,
but the way of the wicked you thwart.
Yahweh shall reign forever—
your God, O Zion, through all generations. Alleluia.

Praise

As we remember those who have passed before us in faith, we give praise to God for the gift of eternal life, as we pray: *Hold us in your loving embrace, God of mercy and kindness.*

- We glorify God who has not abandoned us to the sting of death, as we pray . . .
- We give praise to God for the light of immortality, Christ Jesus, as we pray . . .
- We are filled with wonder at Christ's resurrection, which sets free all people of faith, as we pray . . .
- We are moved with gratitude for the love of God, which has conquered the gates of hell, as we pray . . .
- We remember with gratitude the following people who now reside with God, the creator and redeemer (pause to recall the faithful departed), as we pray . . .
- (Other spontaneous prayers of petition or praise) . . .

Closing

God of the living and the dead, we praise you for the death and resurrection of Christ. As we remember those who have gone before us in faith, we pray for their journey toward the peace of heaven. May they remember us who continue to walk this pilgrim path to the promise of eternal life. We ask this through Christ our light and salvation. Amen.

EVENING

Thanksgiving

All praise and thanks be yours, God of glory
   for the brightness of Christ,
   which has vanquished the darkness of death and sin.
In Christ, the tombs of the dead were broken open,
   and the power of death destroyed.
As we come to dusk,
   we remember those who have passed from this world
   and dwell in the rest and peace of heaven.
We keep their memory still
   and long for their continued joy.
In Christ, our hearts dance before the veil of death
   and hope for that day
   when we shall see you as you are.
All praise and honor be yours
   through Christ and the Holy Spirit
   forever and ever. Amen.

Psalm 116

I love you, Yahweh, because you have heard
   my voice and my supplications,
because you have inclined your ear to me.
Therefore I will call on you as long as I live.
The cords of death encompassed me;
   the pangs of Sheol laid hold on me;
I suffered sorrow and anguish.
Then I called on your name, Yahweh:
"Oh Yahweh, I beseech you, save my life!"
Gracious are you, Yahweh, and righteous;
   you are full of compassion.
You protect the simplehearted;
   when I was brought low, you saved me.
Be at rest once more, O my soul,
   for Yahweh has been good to you.
For you, Yahweh, have delivered my soul from death,
   my eyes from tears,
   my feet from stumbling.
I walk before you, Yahweh,
   in the land of the living.

(Vv. 1–9)

As we remember the faithful departed, we offer our needs to the God of life, as we pray: *Keep us mindful of your love.*

- For the church, that we may proclaim eternal life in the face of death, let us pray . . .
- For every nation, that all people may be liberated from the tombs of oppression, let us pray . . .
- For our community, that our life may be a constant witness to the hope of eternal life, let us pray . . .
- For those people in the throes of sorrow, that they may have the Mother of Sorrows and an angel of mercy to comfort them, let us pray . . .
- For all the dead, that they are cherished in the embrace of God, who is all gentleness and comfort, let us pray . . .
- (Other spontaneous prayers of intercession or contrition, or an examination of conscience) . . .

Intercessions

God of the living and the dead, we praise you for the death and resurrection of Christ. As we remember those who have gone before us in faith, we pray for their journey toward the peace of heaven. May they remember us who continue to walk this pilgrim path to the promise of eternal life. We ask this through Christ our light and salvation. Amen.

Closing